an illustrated introduction to

THE SECOND WORLD WAR

Henry Buckton

AMBERLEY

German soldiers flying a Heinkel He 111P. (Courtesy of the Amberley archives)

First published 2014

Amberley Publishing
The Hill, Stroud
Gloucestershire, GL5 4EP

www.amberley-books.com

British Library Cataloguing in Publication Data.
A catalogue record for this book is available from the British Library.

ISBN 978 1 4456 3848 5 (paperback)
ISBN 978 1 4456 3852 2 (ebook)

Typesetting and Origination by Amberley Publishing.
Printed in Great Britain.

CONTENTS

Using an underground station as a bomb shelter. (Courtesy of the Library of Congress)

THE SECOND WORLD WAR *IN FIVE MINUTES*

The Second World War is so far the only truly global war in history and its causes can be traced back to the end of the First World War. It is generally considered to have started in September 1939 and finished in August 1945, although some historians regard conflicts in Asia that had been going on before this as being part of it.

It involved all of the world's great powers and the vast majority of other nations as well. The participants were, in the main, sided with either one of two opposing military alliances. These were known as the Allies, which included Great Britain, the United States and the Soviet Union, and the Axis, including Germany, Italy and Japan.

It was certainly the most widespread war in history, fought over more of the world's land surface and waters than any other. More than 100 million people, from over thirty different countries, served in uniform and in some countries the vast majority of civilians were also involved in some kind of war work. Most of the major powers waged what was known as 'total war', in which they concentrated their entire industrial, economic and scientific capabilities behind it, erasing the distinction between civilian and military resources.

Perhaps most significantly it was marked by the enormous loss of life, now estimated at around 80 million, which includes 6 million Jews alone killed in the Holocaust. It also saw some of the most destructive advances ever made in defence capabilities and remains the only conflict in which nuclear weapons have been used. All of this made the Second World War the deadliest conflict of all time, and in this book we shall look at all the major events up to and during it, year by year.

After the end of the First World War the political map in Europe was rewritten, with the rise of several fascist states including Italy, where Benito Mussolini came to power, and Germany, where the Nazi Party led by Adolf Hitler took control. The Nazis planned to take back areas which they had lost at the end of the First

World War. They also set about invading other countries to incorporate them into the Third Reich and provide land for German settlers. At first the Allies did little to stop them, but inevitably this expansion would lead to war.

Germany's invasion of Poland in September 1939 was the final straw for France and Britain, who saw no alternative but to declare war, which they had promised the Polish government they would do under such circumstances. Britain sent troops to the Continent but was slow to engage in military action, leading to a period of stalemate which became known as the Phoney War. Germany continued its aggression in the early months of 1940, when they launched attacks on Denmark and Norway followed by assaults on France, Belgium and Holland. They attacked with lightning speed and quickly overran all of these countries.

In the summer of 1940 only Great Britain and its Commonwealth allies were left undefeated. If Germany could invade and conquer Britain, they would win the war. But in order to successfully invade the country they would first have to win air supremacy over the landing beaches. This situation led to the Battle of Britain between July and the end of October 1940, when the German Air Force attempted to defeat the Royal Air Force, which they were unable to do, and by the end of the year Hitler had to cancel the invasion. Nazi Germany had suffered its first military defeat but more importantly, the British Isles could now be used by the Allies to train and equip an army ready for the reconquest of Europe.

Italy had entered the war on the side of the Germans and began to invade other countries, notably Greece and parts of North Africa. Their campaign in Greece ended in failure and the Nazis were forced to come to their assistance in early 1941. The Germans also sent troops to the African deserts, where over the next couple of years they fought several campaigns. They were beaten soundly at the Battle of El Alamein in October 1942, and finally expelled from the continent in May 1943.

Without question Hitler's most ambitious plan was the invasion of the Soviet Union, which began in 1941. But even though the Germans made quick advances into this vast land, the campaign would ultimately bring about their downfall. The enormity of the country, the brutality of its winters and the determination of its people proved to be too much for the invaders. In 1943, following the battles of Stalingrad and Kursk, they were forced into a full retreat with the Russians pursuing them across Eastern Europe and back into Germany itself.

While all of this was taking place war also broke out in the Pacific, when Japan attacked British and American bases on 7 December 1941, most famously the US fleet at Pearl Harbor. This act of aggression brought the United States into the war on all fronts. Japan had already been at war with China but now began a massive campaign of expansion throughout the Far East.

By the middle of 1942 America was ready to react fully and sent a vast army to Britain to prepare for the second front in Europe. But although the priority was given to defeating Germany, America also began naval actions against the Japanese, which climaxed at the Battle of Midway in June 1942, where the Japanese suffered a catastrophic defeat.

For the next year, the United States engaged Japan in a protracted struggle for the Solomon Islands, which lay near vital Allied shipping routes. Between August 1942 and February 1943, Allied forces carried out an invasion on the island of Guadalcanal, which was the start of a series of offensives that would eventually force the Japanese back to their homeland and out of all the island groups they had previously conquered. In the meantime, British and Indian forces were combating Japanese troops in Burma.

By June 1944, British, American, Canadian and other Allied troops were ready to launch the invasion of Europe. On D-Day, 6 June, the Allies assaulted and captured the beaches of Normandy. Shortly afterwards, the German Army in the west was being pushed back towards the Rhine. By early 1945, Allied forces were closing in on Germany from both east and west. The Soviets were the first to reach the German capital of Berlin and Germany surrendered in May 1945, shortly after the suicide of Adolf Hitler.

Although the war in Europe was over, in Asia it continued, with major battles at Leyte, Iwo Jima and Okinawa. By the late spring of 1945, most of Japan's conquests had been liberated, and Allied forces were closing in on the Japanese home islands. As they drew nearer, the Allies carried out a ferocious bombing campaign against major Japanese cities, including Tokyo. This process continued through the summer of 1945 until finally, in early August, the United States dropped two atomic bombs on the cities of Hiroshima and Nagasaki. The Japanese were powerless to resist and surrendered a few days later, bringing the Second World War to a close.

TIMELINE

- **1 September 1939**

  Germany invades Poland, and Britain and France declare war on Germany two days later.

- **May 1940**

  Germany launches the blitzkrieg – lightning attacks in France, Belgium and Holland.

- **10 May 1940**

  Winston Churchill becomes Prime Minister of Britain.

- **May – June 1940**

  Remnants of the British Expeditionary Force are evacuated from Dunkirk.

- **July – October 1940**

  Germany suffers its first defeat during the Battle of Britain.

- **22 June 1941**

  Germany invades the Soviet Union.

- **7 December 1941**

  Japan attacks Pearl Harbor and the United States enters the war.

- **October 1942**

  German Army defeated in the Western Desert at El Alamein.

- **February 1942**

  Singapore surrenders to the Japanese with around 25,000 British prisoners taken.

- **June 1942**

  American Navy defeats a Japanese fleet at the Battle of Midway.

- **31 January 1943**

  German Army surrenders at Stalingrad.

- **May 1943**

  The Axis is finally defeated in North Africa.

- 9 July 1943

  The Allies invade Sicily.
- 3 September 1943

  The Allies invade the Italian mainland.
- 22 January 1944

  The Allies land at Anzio.
- 6 June 1944

  D-Day: the Allies invade Normandy in France.
- July 1944

  The first Jewish concentration camps are liberated by Soviet troops as the extent of the Holocaust is realised.
- 20 April – 2 May

  The Battle of Berlin.
- 30 April 1945

  Adolf Hitler commits suicide.
- 7 May 1945

  Germany surrenders.
- August 1945

  Atomic bombs dropped on Hiroshima (6 August) and Nagasaki (9 August).
- 2 September 1945

  Japan signs the instrument of surrender aboard the USS *Missouri*, officially bringing the Second World War to an end.

Previous page: Soldiers using an MG 34 machine gun. (Courtesy of the Amberley archives)

Above: American B-17 Flying Fortress bombers during a daylight raid over Germany. (© Paul Chryst)

1
1919–1939: THE ROAD TO WAR

In this chapter we shall see how the political scene in Europe changed after the First World War, giving rise to fascist governments in countries like Italy and Germany. We will also study how these new states set forth on a course of empire building and fought military actions which would ultimately have a bearing on the outbreak of the Second World War, while in the Far East, Japan's invasion of China is regarded by many as the true starting point of the greatest global conflict in history.

THE POLITICAL MAP AFTER THE FIRST WORLD WAR

The First World War, or 'Great War' as it was known at the time, ended for Britain with the general Armistice in November 1918 and the signing of the Treaty of Versailles in June 1919. The political map, especially in Europe, was radically changed, with Germany, Austria-Hungary and the Ottoman Empire most affected. Another big change had been the seizure of power in Russia by the Bolsheviks in 1917, and from the collapse of these pre-war powers many of the victorious allies gained new territories.

Inspired by the communist revolt in Russia, a revolution had taken place in Germany at the very end of the war that resulted in the replacement of Germany's imperial government with a republic. Shortly afterwards, Emperor Wilhelm II abdicated, and in August 1919 the new democratic government was formally established and became known as the Weimar Republic.

In Britain in the aftermath of the First World War there was a rise in pacifism as people dreamed of a lasting peace. Adversely, in some of the countries that had been defeated, and in their eyes humiliated, including Germany, there was a surge in irredentist and revanchist nationalism in which they advocated the annexation of territories administered by other states on the grounds of common ethnicity or prior historical possession.

Under the terms of the Treaty of Versailles, Germany had lost approximately 13 per cent of its home territory as well as all of its overseas colonies. The treaty

Signatories to the Treaty of Versailles sit in the Hall of Mirrors in the Palace of Versailles near Paris, on 28 June 1919. (Courtesy of Michael Virtue, Virtue Books)

also imposed reparations and a limit on the size and capability of the country's armed forces.

THE RISE OF THE FASCIST STATES

The first fascist movements emerged in Italy around the time of the First World War. They were hostile towards democracy, socialism and communism, but wherever they emerged they shared certain similarities, including their veneration of the state, devotion to a strong leader and an emphasis on ultra-nationalism and militarism. Fascism viewed political violence, war and imperialism as a means to achieving national rejuvenation and asserted that stronger nations had the right to expand their territory by displacing those that were weaker than themselves.

Although Italy had sided with Britain and its allies during the war and had made some territorial gains on its conclusion, Italian fascists led by Benito Mussolini felt that their country's ambitions had not been fulfilled by the peace settlement. In 1922 Mussolini became Prime Minister of Italy, bringing his National Fascist Party into office. He ruled constitutionally until 1925, when he set up a legal dictatorship which pursued an aggressive foreign policy aimed at transforming Italy into a world power. Mussolini saw himself as the head of a new Roman Empire with the title Il Duce, which meant 'The Leader'.

Meanwhile, in Germany the interwar period was not proving easy for the new Weimar Republic and its legitimacy would soon be challenged by right-wing parties, including the fascist National Socialist German Workers' Party (the Nazi Party) headed by Adolf Hitler, resulting in a number of attempts at deposing it such as the Kapp Putsch and the Beer Hall Putsch.

The Kapp Putsch was an attempted coup in March 1920 aimed at establishing a right-wing autocratic government in place of the Weimar Republic. It took place in the capital, Berlin, forcing the legitimate government to flee. However it failed after only a few days when large sections of the German population followed a Weimar appeal to join a general strike and refused to cooperate with the usurpers.

The Beer Hall Putsch on the other hand was an attempt by the Nazi Party leader, Adolf Hitler, to seize power in Munich in November 1923. Around 2,000 men marched to the city centre and in the ensuing confrontation sixteen Nazis and four policemen were killed. Hitler was arrested and charged with treason. But the failure of the putsch brought Hitler his first significant publicity, and after a trial lasting for twenty-four days he was sentenced to five years in prison. However, he was released after serving only nine months of his sentence.

ADOLF HITLER COMES TO POWER IN GERMANY

Although a failure, the Beer Hall Putsch and Hitler's incarceration all helped the Nazi propaganda machine, so when Germany was affected by the Great Depression of 1929 and its economy collapsed, the people looked towards Hitler and his nationalistic agenda for the answer to their problems. He was appointed Chancellor of Germany in 1933, and in the aftermath of the Reichstag fire, an arson attack on the German seat of parliament in Berlin, created a totalitarian single-party state ruled by the Nazis.

The Nazis claimed the Reichstag fire was the work of German communists, who were their principal political rivals. As chancellor, Hitler urged the Weimar president Paul von Hindenburg to pass an emergency decree to suspend civil liberties in order to counter the communist threat. There were mass arrests of known communists, including all parliamentary delegates. So with their bitterest rivals eliminated, the National Socialist German Workers' Party suddenly found itself in a majority, and Hitler was able to create his Nazi state.

Now that Hitler was effectively the head of the German state, he began to introduce his radical and racially motivated revision of the world order.

Openly flaunting the restrictions of the Treaty of Versailles, he began a massive rearmament campaign and introduced conscription. He also set in motion his plan to take back German territories from those who had benefited from them after the First World War. The first of these was the Saar Basin in early 1935. It was at this time that multiple political analysts began to predict that a second world war was now almost inevitable.

GERMANY RECLAIMS THE SAARLAND

Under the Treaty of Versailles, the highly industrialised Saarland was occupied and governed jointly by the United Kingdom and France under a League of Nations mandate. Its coalfields were also ceded to France. After fifteen years a plebiscite was promised, which was a type of referendum that would determine its future status.

In the 1930s a considerable number of political opponents of the Nazis moved to the Saarland, as it was the only part of Germany that remained under foreign occupation. As a result, anti-Nazi groups agitated for it to remain under British and French occupation. However, as most of the region's population was German, the mandate was unpopular and the promised plebiscite was held on 13 January 1935 with over 90 per cent of the vote in favour of rejoining the German Reich.

Although Hitler had won back the Saarland legally the situation alarmed the Allied powers, who did not believe that this would be the end of his ambitions. They were particularly concerned that Austria would be Hitler's next target. So in an attempt to contain Germany, the countries of Britain, France and surprisingly Italy formed the Stresa Front. The aim of their agreement was to ensure that Germany would be unable to force any changes to the treaties of Versailles and Locarno and to support the independence of Austria. However, much of the Allied agreement was rendered unworkable in June 1935, when the United Kingdom made an independent naval agreement with Germany that eased some of the restrictions placed on it.

The Soviet Union, concerned by Germany's threat to acquire vast areas of Eastern Europe and repopulate it with German nationals, signed a treaty of mutual assistance with France, while on the other side of the Atlantic the United States of America, who had been another of the Western Allies during the First World War, passed the Neutrality Act in August 1935 in an attempt to stay out of any potential escalation.

Right: British troops police the Saarland at the time of the promised plebiscite, while Nazi swastikas fly ominously overhead. (Courtesy of Michael Virtue, Virtue Books)

Below: President Franklin D. Roosevelt signs the Neutrality Act in the White House, determined to keep the USA out of a European war. (Courtesy of Michael Virtue, Virtue Books)

REMILITARISATION OF THE RHINELAND

Under the Treaty of Versailles Germany was forbidden to maintain fortifications or field troops either on the left bank of the River Rhine or within 50 kilometres of its right bank, an area known as the Rhineland. Furthermore, this whole area would be classed as a demilitarised zone. Any violation of this would be regarded as committing a hostile act and the Allies would be obliged to react.

On 7 March 1936, in contravention to the treaty, German forces marched into the Rhineland. This was a huge gamble for Hitler and could have gone badly for him if the French and British had reacted. But they did not, and soon more than 32,000 soldiers and armed policemen had entered the restricted zone.

The reason why the Allies did not react remains cloudy. France was going through an internal political crisis at the time and had little interest in this sideshow, while the British generally supported the view that the section of the Versailles Treaty covering this incursion was unenforceable and agreed that, in this instance, Germany was behaving in a reasonable manner.

Hitler later commented that this had been one of the most nerve-racking forty-eight hours of his life, but from this episode he had learned that as far as Britain was concerned there was certainly room for negotiation with regards to Versailles.

ITALIAN INVASION OF ETHIOPIA

Much of North Africa had traditionally been the colonial chessboard of Britain and France, but now the new Italian fascist regime wished to expand overseas and carve out its own empire. It already had territory in Somaliland and so turned its attention to Ethiopia (also known as Abyssinia), which it invaded in October 1935. Britain and France did little to prevent the invasion, as they were keen to keep Italy as an ally. Germany, on the other hand, was the only major European nation that openly supported the move, and Italy subsequently dropped its own objections to Germany's goal of absorbing Austria.

Italy's justification for the attack was an incident during December 1934 between Italian Somali and Ethiopian troops at the Walwal Oasis on the border between the territories of the two nations, where almost 200 soldiers died. Although both parties were exonerated, Mussolini felt that Ethiopia should have been held accountable, so he used this as a reason to invade the country. He also saw it as an opportunity to provide land for Italians and acquire rich mineral resources to help fight off the effects of the Great Depression.

The war lasted until May 1936, when Ethiopia was annexed into the colony of Italian East Africa. Politically, it is best remembered for exposing the weakness of the League of Nations. Both countries were member states, yet the league failed to control Italy or protect Ethiopia.

SPANISH CIVIL WAR

Following on from its campaign in the Horn of Africa, Italy would enjoy further military action when a civil war broke out in Spain in July 1936. More alarmingly, so would Germany – ignoring all the restrictions placed on it, it had built up one of the largest and best-equipped military forces on the Continent.

Hitler and Mussolini came out in support of the fascist nationalist forces led by General Francisco Franco against the existing government, the Soviet-backed Spanish Republic. Italy and Germany would use the conflict to test new weapons and methods of warfare, and in October 1936 they formed the Rome–Berlin Axis. A month later, Germany and Japan signed the Anti-Comintern Pact, which Italy would also later join.

On 26 April 1937, an event would occur that proved to be a foretaste of what lay ahead for London and other British cities during the Second World War. Franco invited his fascist allies to attack the small town of Guernica, which was the spiritual capital of the Basque people in the north of Spain. The Condor Legion of the German Air Force (Luftwaffe) and the Italian Air Force (Aviazione Legionaria) carried out Operation *Rugen*, an aerial attack which caused widespread destruction and many civilian deaths. The bombing is considered the first substantial raid in aviation history on a civilian target, although Madrid had been bombed several times previously to a lesser extent.

The nationalists won the civil war in April 1939, but during the Second World War Spain remained neutral, and even though Franco sent volunteers to fight on the Eastern Front under German command he did not permit either side to use Spanish territory.

JAPANESE INVASION OF MANCHURIA

While the fascist rulers of Germany and Italy set about their respective empire building, the third country in the Axis, Japan, was set on a similar course in the Far East. Its militaristic government viewed the occupation of China as the first step toward what they considered their country's right to rule Asia.

Japan needed a legitimate excuse to begin hostilities, and found it courtesy of the Mukden Incident, which occurred on 18 September 1931, when a small quantity of dynamite exploded close to a railroad owned by Japan's South Manchuria Railway near the city of Mukden, now known as Shenyang. Although the explosion was too weak to destroy any lines and had been carried out by the Japanese themselves, the Imperial Japanese Army accused Chinese dissidents of the act and responded with a full invasion that led to the occupation of Manchuria. Here Japan established a puppet state called Manchukuo, but after the truth was exposed to the international community it led to Japan's diplomatic isolation and withdrawal from the League of Nations.

Chinese forces subsequently fought several battles against the Japanese invaders, notably in Shanghai, Rehe and Hebei, before the signing of the Tanggu Truce on 31 May 1933, which resulted in Chinese recognition of the existence of Manchukuo by the Kuomintang government. This provided a temporary ceasefire between China and Japan, and for a brief period relations between the two countries improved. On 17 May 1935, the Japanese legation in China was raised to the status of embassy and on 10 June 1935, the He–Umezu Agreement was concluded. Under the agreement China gave Japan virtual control over the province of Hebei. The agreement had been brokered in secret and when its details were leaked to the press, it caused an upsurge in anti-Japanese feelings in China.

The reality was that the agreement gave Chiang Kai-shek, who was the leader of the Kuomintang government, time to concentrate his efforts against the Chinese Communist Party, with which he had been waging a civil war even before the Japanese incursion. But unfortunately Japanese ambitions towards China remained, and this proved to be a temporary respite until hostilities re-erupted with the start of the Second Sino-Japanese War in 1937.

JAPAN INVADES THE REST OF CHINA

In July 1937, Japan captured the former Chinese imperial capital of Beijing after instigating the Marco Polo Bridge Incident. Under agreements going back to the beginning of the century, countries with legations in China, such as Japan, had the right to keep troops there in modest numbers. Small numbers of both Japanese and Chinese soldiers were stationed near the Marco Polo Bridge outside the town of Wanping.

What happened that night is unclear, but the Japanese were undergoing training without giving the customary notice and a few shots were exchanged between them and Chinese troops. Japanese infantry then tried to force their way into Wanping but were driven back. Both sides sent more troops to the area, and early in the morning of 8 July Japanese infantry and armoured vehicles took the bridge but were driven off again.

Attempts were made to calm things down, but the incident gave Japan the excuse to mount a full-scale invasion of China and hundreds of thousands of troops arrived. Beijing and Shanghai both fell in 1937, as did Nanking, where Chiang Kai-Shek had established his Kuomintang capital.

During the invasion the Japanese committed numerous atrocities. As many as 200,000 Chinese may have been slaughtered in the so-called Rape of Nanking. Some of the victims were buried, burned or drowned alive, others dismembered alive.

The British Prime Minister Neville Chamberlain (right), meets Adolf Hitler (second from right), during the Munich Agreement summit. The agreement was signed on 30 September 1938 but dated the 29th. (Courtesy of Michael Virtue, Virtue Books)

THE MUNICH AGREEMENT

In Europe, Germany and Italy were becoming bolder. In March 1938, Germany finally annexed Austria, again provoking little response from other European powers. Encouraged, Hitler began pressing German claims on the Sudetenland, an area of Czechoslovakia with a predominantly ethnic German population. Britain and France both followed the counsel of British Prime Minister Neville Chamberlain and conceded this territory to Germany in the Munich Agreement, which was made against the wishes of the Czechoslovakian government, in exchange for a promise of no further territorial demands by the Germans. Following the summit, Chamberlain famously returned to Great Britain and declared that the Munich Agreement had secured 'peace for our time'.

German soldiers with a Pak gun in position. (Courtesy of the J&C McCutcheon collection)

2

1939: THE OUTBREAK OF WAR

In 1939 Germany continued to break the treaties and agreements it had made after the First World War. It also continued to reoccupy territories over which it believed it had some legitimate claim, but when its troops finally entered Poland it was a push too far, leaving Britain and France no alternative but to declare war.

GERMANY INVADES CZECHOSLOVAKIA

Although Hitler's demands had seemingly been satisfied by the Munich Agreement, in March 1939 Germany invaded the remainder of Czechoslovakia and subsequently split it into the German protectorate of Bohemia and Moravia, and a pro-German client state, the Slovak Republic.

In spite of this provocation, Britain and France still did relatively little to remonstrate, but then Hitler issued demands on the free city of Danzig, which was a semi-autonomous state within Poland occupied mainly by Germans. Alarmed at this, France and Britain gave their guarantee to support Poland if their territory was violated. Similarly, when Italy conquered Albania in April 1939 the same guarantee was extended to Romania and Greece.

Shortly after the Franco-British pledge to Poland had been made, Germany and Italy formalised their own alliance with the Pact of Steel. Hitler then renounced the Anglo-German Naval Agreement and the German–Polish Non-Aggression Pact. He then presented Poland with new terms and agreed to recognise the country's borders if it granted Danzig to Germany. The Poles declined the offer as they felt the city was vital for their own security.

JAPANESE WAR IN MONGOLIA

After the creation of the state of Manchukuo, Japan turned its attentions to Soviet territory that was on its new border. The first serious incident between the

Nazi troops march through Prague, the capital of Czechoslovakia, in March 1939. (Courtesy of Michael Virtue, Virtue Books)

two, the Battle of Lake Khasan, was fought in 1938, and proved a victory for the Russians although the Japanese asserted that it had actually been an inconclusive draw.

In 1939 the Mongolian People's Republic was a communist state allied to the Soviet Union. The Japanese insisted that the border between Manchukuo and Mongolia was the Khalkha River, but the Soviets maintained that it actually ran some sixteen kilometres east of the river. On 11 May a Mongolian cavalry unit entered the disputed area, but was driven back across the river by the Japanese.

Both sides began to build up forces, and soon Japan had 30,000 men in the area. The Soviets sent a new commander, Georgy Zhukov, who brought considerably more motorised and armoured forces to the combat zone, along with a substantial air force.

On 27 June the Japanese attacked the Soviet air base at Tamsak-Bulak in Mongolia. But the strike had not been sanctioned by army headquarters in Tokyo, so in an effort to prevent the situation from escalating Tokyo ordered that no further Soviet air bases should be attacked without their permission first.

ATTACKS AND COUNTER-ATTACKS IN THE FAR EAST

Soviet and Mongolian forces continued to build up on both sides of the Khalkha River. Then the commander of the Japanese Army, Lieutenant General Komatsubara, received the order he had been longing for: 'Expel the invaders.' His plan was for a two-pronged assault but, pre-empting the strike, Zhukov launched a counter-attack with 450 tanks and armoured cars. His force nearly encircled the Japanese, who were forced to withdraw on 5 July.

Shortly afterwards on 23 July the Japanese launched a new attack, this time on Soviet forces defending the Kawatama Bridge. Their artillery laid down an awesome barrage that consumed more than half of their ammunition supplies in just two days. Although the attack made some progress it failed to break through the Soviet lines, and so, because of mounting losses, the Japanese called the attack off on 25 July, having lost some 5,000 men.

The Japanese planned a third major offensive for 24 August, but Zhukov pre-empted them again. He was keen to end the fighting in Mongolia as soon as possible, as a war in Europe seemed increasingly likely. On 20 August Soviet artillery and a massive air armada of 557 fighter and bomber aircraft attacked Japanese positions. With the enemy pinned down by the bombing, Soviet armoured units swept around the flanks and attacked them in the rear, achieving a classic double envelopment. Although the Japanese refused to surrender, by 31 August their forces had been effectively destroyed.

Komatsubara refused to accept the outcome and prepared a counteroffensive, but this was cancelled when a ceasefire was signed in Moscow. While Zhukov had been combating Japanese forces in Mongolia, Joseph Stalin, the General Secretary of the Central Committee of the Communist Party of the Soviet Union, had been making a deal with Nazi Germany called the Molotov–Ribbentrop Pact, which was announced on 24 August. Thereafter the Japanese decided to concentrate their efforts in China and also turn their military attention southward, towards US and European holdings in the Pacific.

THE BRINK OF WAR

The Molotov–Ribbentrop Pact was a non-aggression treaty in which Germany and the Soviet Union agreed to each other's rights to 'spheres of influence'. This basically meant that Germany could invade western Poland and Lithuania without Soviet interference, as long as Germany had no objection to Russia's claims on eastern Poland, Finland, Estonia, Latvia and Bessarabia. For Hitler this was crucial, as it meant that Germany would not have to fight a war on two fronts after it invaded Poland.

Hitler ordered the attack on Poland to start on 26 August, but upon hearing that Britain and France had agreed a mutual assistance pact with Poland and that Italy would remain neutral, he decided to delay it. Britain pleaded for negotiations to try and stop the attack, but Hitler demanded that Poland send a plenipotentiary to Berlin to discuss the handover of Danzig and the Polish Corridor to Germany, as well as to agree to safeguard the German minority in Poland. The Poles refused to comply with this request, and on the evening of 31 August Germany declared that it considered its proposals rejected.

War Breaks out in Europe

On 1 September 1939 troops from Germany and the Slovak Republic invaded Poland. Two days later on 3 September, France and Britain, followed by the dominions of the British Commonwealth, declared war on Germany. However, in the first instance they made little military response other than a small French attack into the Saarland. Britain and France also began a naval blockade of Germany aimed at damaging the country's ability to wage war. Germany responded by ordering U-boat attacks against Allied ships, both merchant and military.

Britain also sent troops to the Continent comprising the British Expeditionary Force. This was a home-based regular army garrisoned at Aldershot under the command of Lieutenant General Sir John Dill. It had been created in 1938 to enable Britain to respond quickly in the event of war with Germany. The first ships left Southampton on 9 September, and by March the following year 316,000 men had been transported. They were mainly deployed along the border between France and Belgium. Units of the Royal Air Force were also dispatched.

On 17 September the Soviets invaded Poland from the east, while in the west the Polish army was defeated in Warsaw and surrendered to the Germans on 27 September. Final pockets of resistance held out until 6 October. Poland was then divided between Germany and the Soviet Union, with Lithuania and Slovakia also receiving small shares. The Poles established an underground state with an underground army, and continued to fight alongside the Allies on many fronts.

On 6 October Hitler made a public peace overture to Britain and France, but said that the future of Poland was to be determined exclusively by Germany and the Soviet Union. Chamberlain rejected this on 12 October, saying, 'Past experience has shown that no reliance can be placed upon the promises of the present German Government.' After this rejection Hitler ordered an immediate offensive against France, but his generals persuaded him to wait until May 1940.

THE EVACUATION SCHEME

It was rightly feared that in the event of war, Germany's attack on Britain would include the indiscriminate bombing of civilian targets, and because of this, some time prior to hostilities, the British government drew up plans to evacuate schoolchildren and some other categories of people from what were considered to be endangered zones. The plan was to move evacuees from the cities to areas of safe haven in the countryside, such as the West Country, Wales and Yorkshire. Much of the work on the ground was organised and undertaken by local authorities and the Women's Voluntary Service. The first evacuation commenced on 1 September 1939, and within four days more than 1.3 million individuals had been moved out of London alone, with other large cities also involved. Children left their homes heading into the unknown, carrying little more than their gas mask and a suitcase.

Officially, there were four groups of people evacuated – schoolchildren, accompanied only by their teachers; mothers with young children; expectant mothers and others with medical problems; and the blind, crippled and mentally ill.

During the course of the entire war there were three principal periods of evacuation. The first, as already mentioned, began just before the declaration. The second was at the start of the London Blitz in September 1940. This occurred because most of the original evacuees had returned home in the interim as little had happened in terms of bombing civilian targets. The third major outflow happened on the advent of the flying bomb attacks in June 1944, because once again many people had drifted back after the end of the heavy raids in May 1941. But having said that, many evacuees remained with their new foster families for the duration of the war, and although this led to many cases of abuse, for others it was a time of many happy memories.

Left: Children being evacuated. (Courtesy of Michael Virtue, Virtue Books)

Below: Civilians welcome a British contingent of the BEF as it travels through a Belgian town on its way to the front line. (Courtesy of Michael Virtue, Virtue Books)

THE PHONEY WAR

After the declaration of war very little happened in Western Europe militarily, and this period became known as the Phoney War. This term was first used, allegedly, by an American senator called Borah. Winston Churchill referred to the same period as the twilight war, while the Germans called it the *sitzkrieg* or sitting war. In fact, so little happened that many of the children that had been evacuated from British cities at the start of the war returned home.

But to assume that nothing happened during this period would be wrong, as a number of incidents of note did take place. The sinking of the British passenger vessel the SS *Athenia*, for instance, sent a clear message to Britain that Germany was prepared to sink liners and not just ships of military importance. This happened at 9 a.m. on 3 September, when a U-boat attacked the ship while it was on its way to Canada. The German commander claimed that he believed the *Athenia* was a naval boat as it was sailing in a zigzag manner, and in the poor light he could not differentiate between a liner and a naval vessel. Of the 1,103 passengers and 315 crew aboard, 115 died.

On 14 October 1939, the British battleship HMS *Royal Oak* was anchored at Scapa Flow in Orkney when she was torpedoed by another German submarine. Of *Royal Oak*'s complement of 1,234 men and boys, 833 were killed or died later of their wounds. The daring raid made an immediate hero out of the U-boat commander Gunther Prien, who became the first German submariner to be awarded the Knight's Cross of the Iron Cross. Before the sinking, the Royal Navy had considered the naval base at Scapa Flow impregnable to submarine attack. Many people in Britain first learned about the loss of the *Royal Oak* from the broadcasts of the Nazi propagandist William Joyce, better known as Lord Haw-Haw.

The Germans also began to carry out aerial attacks on British military targets on the mainland. On 16 October they attacked ships of the Royal Navy based at Rosyth in the Firth of Forth. On this occasion the first two enemy aircraft were shot down over mainland Britain, both of which fell into the sea. They were both destroyed by Supermarine Spitfires, the aircraft that would play such an important role in the defence of Britain a year later and put fear into enemy air crews.

During the Phoney War, Britain was also engaged in raids over Germany, but it was not bombs that were dropped but propaganda leaflets. Sir Kingsley Wood, Secretary of State for War, called them 'truth raids' which served to inform the

German populace about the evils of Nazi Germany and to show their leaders just how vulnerable their country was to potential bombing raids.

WARTIME PROPAGANDA

During the Second World War the British Ministry of Information used propaganda as a way of influencing people to support the war effort. Both the United States of America and Germany used similar tactics. They used a wide range of media in order to do this and their principal aims were to increase hatred for the enemy among the general public while at the same time appealing to their sense of patriotism.

What was printed in the newspapers was very much dictated by the government and censored. As well as the press itself, posters were a popular method of spreading propaganda. Less traditional media was also used, such as the making of movies that portrayed the heroics of the British armed forces. These movies were also part of a recruitment drive to get young men into certain branches of the military. Newsreels shown in cinemas portrayed genuine British troops fighting around the world and were largely accurate in their content, emphasising that propaganda didn't necessarily have to be deceptive. Radio broadcasts by senior politicians, primarily the Prime Minister Winston Churchill, were also used and were hugely popular. Entire families would sit around their wireless at times when the Prime Minister was scheduled to make a speech and these certainly helped to maintain civilian morale and lift spirits. But propaganda also helped in the support of specific pro-war projects such as conserving metal, growing vegetables, selling war bonds and promoting efficiency in factories.

Leaflets were another form of propaganda that would be dropped behind enemy lines by aircraft to try and disrupt the foe, especially following D-Day, when they urged soldiers to defy their leaders, who did not have their interests at heart, and in so doing surrender to the Allies as their position was becoming hopeless. So in many ways, propaganda was a weapon in itself, and was used to help win the war.

The cover of an official wartime booklet about the Home Front, depicting branches of the Civil Defence, is an example of wartime propaganda in print. (Author's collection)

THE WINTER WAR

Following the invasion of Poland, the Soviet Union invaded Finland in November 1939. The resulting Winter War ended with Finnish concessions. France and the United Kingdom, treating the attack as tantamount to entering the war on the side of the Germans, responded to the invasion by supporting the USSR's expulsion from the League of Nations.

In attacking Finland the Soviet Union sought to conquer but also recover an area which had previously been part of the Russian Empire as the Grand Duchy of Finland. The Soviet Union demanded among other concessions that Finland cede substantial border territories, claiming it was for security reasons, mainly the protection of Leningrad, which was only forty kilometres from the Finnish border. Finland refused and the Soviet Union declared war.

At the time the Soviets possessed more than three times as many soldiers as the Finns, thirty times as many aircraft, and a hundred times as many tanks. The Red

Army, however, had been crippled by Joseph Stalin's Great Purge of 1937, when more than 30,000 Russian officers had been executed or imprisoned, including many of high rank, which left it full of inexperienced leaders. Because of these factors, as well as high morale among the Finnish forces, Finland managed to repel Soviet attacks for several months.

However, after reorganisation and adoption of different tactics, the overwhelming numbers of Soviet forces overcame Finnish defences at the borders. Finland then agreed to cede the territory originally demanded by the Soviet Union; the Soviets, having lost far more troops than anticipated, accepted this offer.

Hostilities ceased in March 1940 with the signing of the Moscow Peace Treaty. Finland ceded territory representing 11 per cent of its land area and 30 per cent of its economy to the Soviet Union. Soviet losses were heavy and the country's reputation dented, but although it did not conquer all of Finland, its gains somewhat exceeded its pre-war demands. Finland on the other hand retained its sovereignty and enhanced its international reputation.

BATTLE OF THE RIVER PLATE

In December 1939 Britain won a naval victory over Germany in the South Atlantic known as the Battle of the River Plate, which was to be the first major naval battle in the Second World War and the only episode of the conflict to take place in South America. The German pocket battleship *Admiral Graf Spee* had been commerce raiding since the start of the war, so the British Admiralty sent out hunting groups to search for her. One of these, comprising three Royal Navy cruisers, HMS *Exeter*, HMS *Ajax*, and HMS *Achilles* (the last of the New Zealand Division), found and engaged their quarry off the estuary of the River Plate close to the coast of Argentina and Uruguay in South America.

In the ensuing battle, *Exeter* was severely damaged and forced to retire; *Ajax* and *Achilles* suffered moderate damage. The damage to *Graf Spee* was critical as her fuel system had been crippled. *Ajax* and *Achilles* shadowed the German ship until she entered the port of Montevideo, the capital city of neutral Uruguay, to effect urgent repairs. After *Graf Spee*'s captain, Hans Langsdorff, was told that his stay could not be extended beyond seventy-two hours, he scuttled his damaged ship rather than face the overwhelmingly superior force that the British had led him to believe was awaiting his departure. So as 1939 came to a close, Britain ended the first year of the war with a victory.

3

1940: THE FINEST HOUR

In the early months of 1940 the German Army was in its ascendancy, and with blitzkrieg strikes on countries like Norway and later France, it seemed unstoppable. But then it would suffer its first serious setback in the Battle of Britain, when the fighter pilots of Fighter Command known as 'The Few', as well as everyone else involved, including the Observer Corps, anti-aircraft batteries and those operating the barrage balloons, halted the Nazi juggernaut. Importantly this allowed Britain to fight on alone and provide a platform from which to launch future Allied campaigns.

THE INVASIONS OF DENMARK AND NORWAY

In February 1940 the Soviet Union and Germany agreed on a trade pact, by which the Soviets would receive military and industrial equipment in exchange for raw materials. Germany also imported a lot of iron ore from Sweden, but the Allies were hindering its transportation by mining the channels the shipments crossed, which were actually within the waters of neutral Norway. In order to safeguard the shipments Germany invaded Denmark and Norway on the morning of 9 April. Denmark capitulated after a few hours, but Norway resisted.

The German attack on Norway was code named Operation *Weserubung*, but when their ships entered Oslofjord, their flagship, the *Blucher*, was sunk. *Blucher* had been transporting the forces needed to control the political apparatus in Norway after the invasion, and its sinking delayed the Germans long enough for the King of Norway, Haakon VII, and his government to escape from Oslo.

German paratroopers, the very first ever used in warfare, captured the airfields at Stavanger and Olso, while resistance at Narvik, Trondheim, Bergen, Stavanger and Kristiansand was quickly quashed. But the initial success the Norwegians had in holding off the seaborne assault on Oslo was cancelled out when troops that had landed at the airfield entered the city. Then, having established a foothold along the coast, the Germans launched a ground offensive against inland targets.

Britain and France both sent troops to help Norway, which began to arrive at Narvik on 14 April. They outnumbered the Germans by about five to one and after a stubborn fight the invaders eventually withdrew on 28 May. However, by this time the Germans had launched an offensive in France, and because of this the Allies could not afford to commit any further men to Norway. So their victory at Narvik accounted for nothing as ten days later all Allied troops were evacuated to fight elsewhere.

Fighting continued until 10 June when Norway finally surrendered. But in Britain, discontent over the campaign had led to the replacement of the British Prime Minister, Neville Chamberlain, with Winston Churchill on 10 May.

BLITZKRIEG IN FRANCE

In Poland and Norway the Germans had launched lightning attacks which were known as blitzkrieg. They would employ the same method of warfare in France, which they attacked on 10 May, while simultaneously invading the neutral nations of Belgium, the Netherlands and Luxembourg. On the same day the British occupied the Danish possessions of Iceland, Greenland and the Faroes to prevent them falling into German hands.

The Battle of France consisted of two main operations. In the first, *Fall Gelb* (Case Yellow), German armoured units pushed through the densely wooded Ardennes region, mistakenly perceived by Allied planners as an impenetrable natural barrier. The Allied forces were pushed back to the sea and the British government decided that the best course of action was to evacuate the British Expeditionary Force from the beaches of Dunkirk.

EVACUATION FROM DUNKIRK

By 21 May German forces had trapped the BEF and pushed it back to the sea, while at Lille 40,000 men of the once-formidable French First Army held out until 31 May against seven German divisions.

On the first day of the evacuation from Dunkirk only 7,669 men were extracted, but by the ninth day a total of 338,226 soldiers had been rescued by a hastily assembled fleet of over 800 boats. This number not only included British troops, but French and Belgian also.

Many of the troops embarked from the harbour's protective mole on to British destroyers and other large ships, while others had to wade out from the beaches,

Allied soldiers are seen here being rescued from the beaches of Dunkirk by the armada of little ships. (Courtesy of Michael Virtue, Virtue Books)

waiting for hours in shoulder-deep water. Some were ferried from the beaches to the larger vessels by the famous little ships of Dunkirk, a flotilla of hundreds of merchant marine boats, fishing boats, pleasure craft and lifeboats called into service for the emergency.

The BEF lost 68,000 soldiers during the French campaign and had to abandon nearly all of their tanks, vehicles and other equipment. Some military chiefs and politicians began to call Dunkirk a miracle, but in his speech to the House of Commons on 4 June, Churchill reminded the country that 'we must be very careful not to assign to this deliverance the attributes of a victory. Wars are not won by evacuations.'

THE BATTLE OF FRANCE CONTINUES

After the withdrawal of the BEF, Germany launched a second operation, *Fall Rot* (Case Red), which was commenced on 5 June. While the depleted French put up stiff initial resistance, German air superiority and armoured mobility overwhelmed their remaining forces. German armour outflanked the French-fortified Maginot Line and pushed deep into France. Although most of the fighting was now already over, Italy declared war on France and Britain on 10 June and also invaded France. German forces finally arrived in an undefended Paris on

14 June, which caused a chaotic period of flight for the French government and effectively ended organised French military resistance.

On 22 June, an armistice was signed between France and Germany, which resulted in the division of the country. Germany would occupy the north and west, Italy a small zone in the south-east, and an unoccupied zone would be governed by the newly formed Vichy government led by Prime Minister Marshal Philippe Pétain which, though officially neutral, was generally aligned with Germany.

In June 1940, the Soviet Union forcibly annexed Estonia, Latvia and Lithuania and then annexed the disputed Romanian region of Bessarabia. Meanwhile, Nazi–Soviet political and economic cooperation gradually stalled, and both states began preparations for war with one another.

On 19 July Hitler again publicly offered to end the war, saying he had no desire to destroy the British Empire. Britain rejected this, with Lord Halifax responding that 'there was in his speech no suggestion that peace must be based on justice, no word of recognition that the other nations of Europe had any right to self-determination'.

Sinking of the French Fleet

Although the French Army had surrendered, its navy, one of the greatest in the world, remained intact. Churchill was fearful that these ships might fall into Nazi hands even though their commander, Admiral Francois Darlan, insisted that they

German soldiers rush to defend against an air raid by Allied forces. (Courtesy of the Amberley archives)

would not. Churchill was not prepared to take the gamble and tried to convince his war cabinet that attacking the French fleet was their best course. The cabinet were unconvinced at this time as France was still an ally.

As part of the armistice signed between France and Germany, the Vichy government was allowed to keep its ships. Churchill demanded their surrender but after Darlan refused he finally got the backing of his war cabinet and ordered the assault.

On 3 July the British surrounded the French fleet at the port of Mers-el-Kebir outside Oran in Algeria. Churchill sent Darlan a message to sail his ships to Britain or the USA, or scuttle them within six hours. The French showed the British an order they had received from Darlan instructing them to sail the ships to the USA if the Germans broke the armistice and demanded them.

Meanwhile, the British intercepted a message from the Vichy government ordering French reinforcements to move urgently to Oran. Churchill was through playing games and gave the order of attack to his commanders. An hour and a half later the British attacked. In less than ten minutes, 1,297 French soldiers were dead and three battleships were sunk. One battleship and five destroyers managed to escape.

While the French were furious over the events, the reaction in England was the exact opposite. The day after the attack Churchill went to the House of Commons to explain why he had ordered it. For the first time since taking office as Prime Minister, Churchill received a unanimous standing ovation.

THE BATTLE OF BRITAIN

With France defeated and overrun, Britain now stood alone as the Germans arrived on the French coast. Winston Churchill proclaimed that the Battle of France was over and that the Battle of Britain was about to begin. But if Hitler was going to invade Britain his army would have to cross the Channel and land on the beaches of Kent and Sussex. His plan was code named Operation *Sealion*, and its success depended on achieving air superiority. In other words, the Luftwaffe, commanded by Reichsmarschall Hermann Goering, would first have to defeat the Royal Air Force to make sure that they were unable to attack his ships as they crossed the sea and troops as they assaulted the beaches. They also needed total control of the Channel waters, to stop the Royal Navy taking part in the operation.

The force defending Britain was called Fighter Command and was commanded by Air Chief Marshal Sir Hugh Dowding. But although its aircraft and pilots were

Left: A Messerschmitt Bf 109 of the German Air Force shot down over southern England during the Battle of Britain is being removed by men of the RAF. (Courtesy of Michael Virtue, Virtue Books)

Above: In this painting called *The Chase*, a Hurricane of the RAF is seen in pursuit of a German Heinkel He 111 at the height of the Battle of Britain. (© Joe Crowfoot)

gravely outnumbered by the enemy, Britain did have a number of advantages over the Luftwaffe. Most importantly it had Radio Direction Finding (RDF), which later became known as RADAR. This gave Fighter Command early warning of the approach of enemy aircraft, which meant that Dowding and his controllers could direct their Spitfires and Hurricanes to attack them. There was also the Observer Corps (later Royal Observer Corps), which plotted the movement of enemy aircraft when over land from a series of hilltop posts. Nothing moved in the sky over Britain without being spotted by these men and women, and the information they gathered was passed to Fighter Command.

The battle started on 10 July when the Luftwaffe attempted to gain control of the Straits of Dover by attacking convoys of ships. Their aim was to tempt the RAF into the sky for a full-scale battle and destroy it. But by the end of July the Luftwaffe had lost far more aircraft than Fighter Command: 268 to 150.

In August, the Luftwaffe decided to attack Fighter Command on the ground and in so doing destroy airfields, control rooms and radar sites. In doing this they hoped to put their enemy out of business and win air superiority that way. They also attacked aircraft factories such as Supermarine in Southampton, which was making Spitfires. This, they hoped, would stop new aircraft getting to the RAF.

BEGINNING OF THE BLITZ

Just when Fighter Command was at its lowest ebb and facing defeat, on 23 August the Germans changed tactics again and began the Blitz, the night-time bombing of London and other major cities. This was a godsend for the RAF because, although many of its airfields had now been put out of action, they were suddenly in a position to rebuild and regroup.

On 15 September came the last major engagement of the battle. On that day, the Luftwaffe lost sixty planes while the RAF lost twenty-eight. On 17 September Hitler postponed indefinitely the invasion of Britain, although the night raids continued.

The importance of the Battle of Britain cannot be underestimated because if Britain had lost it, the country would have been invaded in 1940 and the war would have been over. Instead, Hitler suffered his first major defeat and the war continued.

Below left: Fire boats of the Auxiliary Fire Service on the Thames during the London Blitz. (Courtesy of Michael Virtue, Virtue Books)

Below right: During the Blitz, although London was the main target of the bombing raids, several other cities were also very badly affected, incluing Portsmouth. This is the cover of a contemporary booklet that illustrated the destruction around the city. (Author's collection)

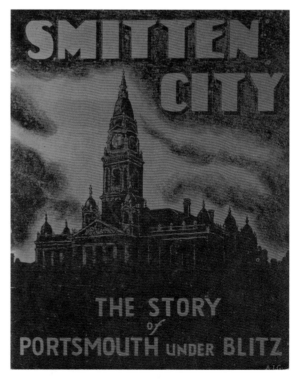

The London Blitz

The Blitz on London was the most ferocious and concerted attack that Britain has ever been subjected to. Night after night, waves of between 200 and 400 bombers would drop high explosives all over the city: at one point this happened for fifty-seven consecutive nights. The aim of the Luftwaffe was to destroy London's infrastructure in one massive knockout blow. They did this by targeting power stations, docks, railways and aerodromes. They also attacked civilian suburbs on a huge and unprecedented scale. Their hope was not only to destroy the city's ability to function, but to demoralise the British people so much that their government would be forced to capitulate.

At the height of the Blitz, between September 1940 and May 1941, over 50,000 high explosive bombs were dropped on London, as well as tens of thousands of incendiary bombs. Some 1.15 million houses were damaged and over 1.4 million people were made homeless. In total, over 41,000 British civilians were killed during the war, and 137,000 injured. Of the dead, 7,736 were children.

The nightly bombing of Britain was not confined to London alone. The systematic destruction of many major cities and towns was attempted, especially those with a heavy industrial base. Southampton, Portsmouth, Plymouth, Bristol, Liverpool, Hull, Coventry, Derby, Leicester, Sheffield, Birmingham, Manchester and Glasgow were among the cities badly affected. In Plymouth one household in four was made homeless, and on Clydebank only seven out of 12,000 homes remained undamaged.

But bombs were dropped all over Britain, not merely on the cities. Some came down in the most unlikely places, and even in remote rural corners. Britain is a relatively small island and most places are not very far from a major urban centre, so many people found themselves living under a flight path used by the Germans to attack Britain's industrial base, and after each air raid the Nazi crews would offload any bombs they had not used anywhere they saw a light.

"ALL CLEAR."

A humorous wartime postcard illustrates the point that some people in the city used underground public conveniences as air-raid shelters. (Author's collection)

THE TRIPARTITE PACT

At the end of September the Tripartite Pact united Japan, Italy and Germany to formalise Axis powers. The pact stipulated that any country not in the war (with the exception of the Soviet Union) that attacked any Axis power would be forced to go to war against all three. The Axis expanded in November 1940 when Hungary, Slovakia and Romania joined the Tripartite Pact.

ACTIONS IN THE MEDITERRANEAN

Italy began operations in the Mediterranean in June 1940, initiating a siege of the British island of Malta. They also invaded and conquered British Somaliland in August and made an incursion into British-held Egypt in September.

In October Italian troops attempted to invade Greece from their bases in Albania, but within days they were repulsed and pushed back across the border, where a stalemate soon occurred. Britain responded to Greek requests for assistance by sending troops to Crete and providing air support. Hitler decided to take action against Greece when the weather improved to assist the Italians and prevent the British from gaining a foothold in the Balkans. He also aimed to strike against the British naval presence in the Mediterranean and secure his hold on Romania's oilfields.

TORPEDO ATTACK ON TARANTO

In mid-1940 the balance of power was starting to tilt against Admiral Cunningham's Mediterranean Fleet of the Royal Navy. The Italians had no fewer than six battleships and outnumbered Cunningham in every class of vessel except aircraft carriers. So the British Fleet Air Arm decided to carry out a daring raid on the Italian fleet at Taranto, their main naval base on the south coast of Italy.

Winston Churchill was anxious that Italian strength be reduced before German forces arrived to bolster their ally, so on 6 November HMS *Illustrious* prepared for Operation *Judgement*, which would take place on the night of 11/12 November. On board were twenty-one Swordfish aircraft which would attack the Italians in two waves: eleven were armed with torpedoes, the remainder carrying flares and bombs.

Although the Italians did not have radar, a patrolling RAF Sunderland flying boat alerted their defences before the Swordfish in the first wave arrived. The aircraft may have been few in number but their crews were highly experienced and the result was catastrophic for the Italians. Five torpedoes struck three battleships, *Littorio*, *Caio Duilio* and *Conte di Cavour*. The attack immediately halved the strength of the Italian battle fleet and the surviving ships took refuge in Naples.

In December 1940, British Commonwealth forces began counteroffensives against Italian forces in Egypt and Italian East Africa. The offensive in North Africa was highly successful and by early February 1941 Italy had lost control of eastern Libya and large numbers of Italian troops had been taken prisoner.

A Fairey Swordfish torpedo bomber of the type used at Taranto is seen flying over a British aircraft carrier. (Courtesy of Michael Virtue, Virtue Books)

4

1941: AMERICA JOINS THE FIGHT

Throughout much of 1941 the Axis powers continued their process of occupying other countries and subjugating the peoples they conquered, often with a heavy and violent hand. However in December the Japanese would attack the United States Pacific Fleet at Pearl Harbor, bringing America into the war, an occurrence that would ultimately lead to the destruction of all the Axis regimes.

GERMAN INVOLVEMENT IN THE MEDITERRANEAN

With things going from bad to worse for the Italians in their various ventures, the Germans decided to intervene and assist their ally. Hitler sent German forces to

On entering the war America immediately sent aircraft and men to Britain. This painting by Joe Crowfoot shows the scene at a Rougham airfield from where the US Air Force bombed enemy targets on the Continent. (Joe Crowfoot)

Libya in February, which by the end of March had launched an offensive against the Commonwealth forces in North Africa. In less than a month the Allied troops had been pushed back into Egypt with the exception of those defending the port of Tobruk, who prepared for a lengthy siege.

By late March, following Bulgaria's signing of the Tripartite Pact, the Germans were in a position to intervene in Greece. But the situation suddenly changed because although neighbouring Yugoslavia had also signed the Tripartite Pact on 25 March, its government was overthrown two days later by a British-encouraged coup. Hitler viewed the new regime as hostile and immediately decided to eliminate it. On 6 April Germany simultaneously invaded both Greece and Yugoslavia, making rapid progress and forcing both nations to surrender within the month; then Crete fell in May. But although the Axis victory had been swift, partisan forces in Yugoslavia decided to keep up the fight, which they continued to do until the end of the war.

ALLIED SUCCESSES

The Allies did have some successes during this time. For instance, between 27 and 29 March the Royal Navy had fought and won the Battle of Cape Matapan. The cape in question is on the south-west coast of Greece's Peloponnesian peninsula. Acting on intercepted signals broken by the Government Code and Cypher School at Bletchley Park, a force of British ships accompanied by several Royal Australian Navy vessels, under the command of Admiral Cunningham, intercepted and sank, or severely damaged, several ships of the Italian Navy.

In the Middle East, Commonwealth forces first quashed an uprising in Iraq which had been supported by German aircraft from bases within Vichy-controlled Syria. Then, with the assistance of the Free French, they invaded Syria and Lebanon to prevent further such occurrences.

SINKING OF THE *BISMARCK*

In the Atlantic Ocean German U-boats were enjoying great success over the Royal and Merchant Navies while operating out of captured ports along the Bay of Biscay coast of France, but on 27 May 1941 the British would score a significant victory by sinking the German flagship *Bismarck* some 560 kilometres west of Brest.

In a sense the battle in which the *Bismarck* was sunk was a sequel to the Battle of the Denmark Strait, fought on 24 May 1941, in which the *Bismarck* and her escort, the heavy cruiser *Prinz Eugen*, had sunk the British battlecruiser HMS *Hood* and damaged the battleship HMS *Prince of Wales*. Following that battle the *Bismarck* was pursued for more than two days by ships and aircraft of the Royal Navy and Royal Air Force. Eventually, on the evening of 26 May, her steering gear was crippled by a torpedo bomber attack, and on the following morning she sank.

THE UNITED STATES WATCHES AND WAITS

Throughout the early stages of the war, the neutral United States took measures to assist China and the Western Allies. In November 1939, the American Neutrality Act was amended to allow cash-and-carry purchases by the Allies. Under the terms of the original act the US was forbidden from supplying weapons to any country involved in a war. Cash and carry is the term applied to an amendment to the act that allowed countries to purchase weapons and war materials from the US provided they were paid for in cash and were transported in the purchasers' own ships.

In 1940, following the capture of Paris, the size of the United States Navy was significantly increased. In September, the United States further agreed to a trade of

President Roosevelt of the United States greets the British Prime Minister Winston Churchill aboard the USS *Augusta* in Placentia Bay on 9 August 1941, for talks that would form the basis of the Atlantic Charter. (Courtesy of Michael Virtue, Virtue Books)

American destroyers for British bases. Even so, a large majority of the American public still continued to oppose any direct military intervention into the conflict well into 1941.

Although President Roosevelt had promised to keep the United States out of the war, he nevertheless took measures to prepare for that eventuality. In December 1940 he accused Hitler of planning world conquest and ruled out negotiations as useless, calling for the US to become an 'arsenal for democracy', and promoted the passage of Lend-Lease aid to support the British war effort. In January 1941 secret high-level staff talks with the British began for the purposes of determining how to defeat Germany should the US enter the war. They decided on a number of policies, including an air offensive, the early elimination of Italy, support for resistance groups, and the capture of areas from where the second front could be implemented.

GERMAN ATTACK ON THE USSR

Hitler believed that Britain's refusal to end the war was based on the hope that the United States and the Soviet Union would enter the war against Germany sooner or later. He therefore decided to try to strengthen Germany's relations with the Soviets, or failing that, to attack and eliminate them as a factor. In November 1940 negotiations had taken place to determine if the Soviet Union would join the Tripartite Pact. The Soviets showed some interest, but asked for concessions from Finland, Bulgaria, Turkey, and Japan that Germany considered unacceptable. On 18 December 1940 Hitler issued the directive to prepare for an invasion of the Soviet Union.

So with tensions rising between Germany and the Soviet Union, and the Japanese planning to seize European possessions in South East Asia, the two powers signed the Soviet–Japanese Neutrality Pact in April.

On 22 June 1941, Germany and Romania invaded the Soviet Union in Operation *Barbarossa*. As an excuse, Germany accused the Soviets of plotting against them. Hitler's troops were joined shortly afterwards by reinforcements from Finland and Hungary. The objectives of this surprise attack were the Baltic region, Moscow and Ukraine, with the goal of ending 1941 along the Arkhangelsk–Astrakhan line, which ran from the Caspian Sea to the White Sea, in the main following the Volga River. As well as destroying the Soviet Union as a military force and exterminating communism, Hitler's plan was to generate *Lebensraum*, which was the provision of living space for German settlers by dispossessing the native population. He also wished to guarantee access to the strategic resources needed to defeat Germany's remaining rivals.

Although the Red Army was preparing for counteroffensives before the war, *Barbarossa* forced them to adopt a strategic defence policy. During the summer, the Axis made significant gains into Soviet territory, inflicting immense losses in both personnel and materiel. The Kiev offensive in particular was extremely successful, paving the way for advances into the Crimea and the industrially developed eastern Ukraine.

The diversion of three-quarters of the Axis troops and the majority of their air forces from France and the central Mediterranean to the Eastern Front prompted Britain to reconsider its grand strategy. In July, the UK and the Soviet Union formed a military alliance against Germany and invaded Iran to secure its oilfields.

By October, when Axis operational objectives in Ukraine and the Baltic region were achieved, with only the sieges of Leningrad and Sevastopol continuing, a major offensive against Moscow had been renewed. After two months of fierce battles, the German Army almost reached the outer suburbs of Moscow, where the exhausted troops were forced to suspend their offensive. Large territorial gains were made by Axis forces, but their campaign had failed to achieve its main objectives: two key cities remained in Soviet hands, the Soviet capability to resist was not broken, and the Soviet Union retained a considerable part of its military potential.

German motorcycle troops such as those shown below were among the forces that invaded Russian territory in June 1941. (Courtesy of the Amberley archives)

By early December, freshly mobilised reserves allowed the Soviets to achieve numerical parity with the Axis. Although they retained a minimal number of troops in the east to prevent an attack by the Japanese, the vast majority of these soldiers were used to launch a massive counteroffensive against the Germans which began on 5 December and which pushed the Nazis back to the west.

THE STRUGGLE FOR CHINA

In 1939 the United States had renounced its trade treaty with Japan, and beginning with an aviation gasoline ban in July 1940, Japan had become subject to increasing economic pressure. Despite several offensives by both sides, the war between China and Japan was stalemated by 1940. In order to increase pressure on China by blocking supply routes, and to better position Japanese forces in the event of a war with the Western powers, Japan had occupied northern Indochina. Afterwards, the United States embargoed iron, steel and mechanical parts against Japan. Other sanctions soon followed.

Chinese communists launched an offensive in central China in August, but in retaliation Japan instituted harsh measures in occupied areas to reduce human and material resources for the communists. Continued antipathy between Chinese communist and nationalist forces culminated in armed clashes in January 1941, effectively ending their cooperation. In September, Japan attempted to take the city of Changsha and clashed with Chinese nationalist forces.

German successes in Europe encouraged Japan to increase pressure on European governments in South East Asia. The Dutch government agreed to provide Japan some oil supplies from the Dutch East Indies, but negotiations for additional access to their resources ended in failure in June 1941. In July Japan sent troops to southern Indochina, thus threatening British and Dutch possessions in the Far East. The United States, United Kingdom and other Western governments reacted to this move with a freeze on Japanese assets and a total oil embargo.

MANOEUVRING IN THE PACIFIC

Since early 1941 the United States and Japan had been engaged in negotiations in an attempt to improve their strained relations and end the war in China. During these negotiations Japan advanced a number of proposals which were dismissed by the Americans as inadequate. At the same time the US, Britain and the Netherlands engaged in secret discussions for the joint defence of their territories in the event of a Japanese attack against any of them. Roosevelt reinforced the Philippines, which had been an American possession since 1898, and warned Japan that the US would react to Japanese attacks against any 'neighboring countries'.

Frustrated at the lack of progress and feeling the pinch of the American–British–Dutch sanctions, Japan prepared for war. On 20 November it presented an interim proposal as its final offer. It called for the end of American aid to China and the supply of oil and other resources to Japan. In exchange they promised not to launch any attacks in South East Asia and to withdraw their forces from their threatening positions in southern Indochina. The American counter-proposal of 26 November required that Japan evacuate all of China without conditions and conclude non-aggression pacts with all Pacific powers. That meant Japan was essentially forced to choose between abandoning its ambitions in China or seizing the natural resources it needed in the Dutch East Indies by force. The Japanese military did not consider the former an option and many officers considered the oil embargo an unspoken declaration of war.

Although America wanted to stay out of the conflict, its military might was already arguably the most formidable in the world. At the time of Pearl Harbor, Japanese Admiral Isoroku Yamamoto is quoted to have said, 'All we have done is to awaken a sleeping giant and fill him with a terrible resolve.' (Courtesy of 4th Division Living History Group)

Japan planned to rapidly seize European colonies in Asia to create a large defensive perimeter stretching into the central Pacific; the Japanese would then be free to exploit the resources of South East Asia while exhausting the overstretched Allies by fighting a defensive war. To prevent American intervention while securing the perimeter it was further planned to neutralise the United States Pacific Fleet and the American military presence in the Philippines from the outset.

Japan attacks the Western Allies

On 7 December (8 December in Asian time zones) 1941, Japan attacked British and American holdings with near-simultaneous offensives against South East Asia and the central Pacific. These included an attack on the American fleet at Pearl Harbor, landings in Thailand and Malaya and the Battle of Hong Kong.

These attacks led the United States, Britain, China, Australia and several other states to formally declare war on Japan, whereas the Soviet Union, being heavily involved in large-scale hostilities with European Axis countries, preferred to maintain a neutrality agreement with Japan.

Attack on Pearl Harbor

The attack on Pearl Harbor by the Imperial Japanese Navy commenced at 7.48 a.m. Hawaiian time. The base was attacked by 353 Japanese fighters, bombers and torpedo planes in two waves, launched from six aircraft carriers. All eight US Navy battleships at the site were damaged, with four being sunk. All but one were later raised, and six of the eight battleships returned to service and fought in the war.

The Japanese also sank or damaged three cruisers, three destroyers, an anti-aircraft training ship, and one minelayer. Some 188 US aircraft were destroyed; 2,402 Americans were killed and 1,282 wounded. Japanese losses were light: twenty-nine aircraft and five midget submarines lost, and sixty-five servicemen killed or wounded.

The attack came as a profound shock to the American people and led directly to the American entry into the war in both the Pacific and European theatres. The following day (8 December), the United States declared war on Japan. Domestic support for non-interventionism, which had been strong, disappeared. Subsequent operations by the US prompted Germany and Italy to declare war on the US on 11 December, which was reciprocated by the US the same day.

The lack of any formal warning before the attack on Pearl Harbor, particularly while negotiations were still apparently ongoing, led President Roosevelt to proclaim 7 December 1941 'a date which will live in infamy'.

Above: Admiral Osami Nagano, commander-in-chief of the Japanese Navy, who directed the attack on the American fleet at Pearl Harbor. (Courtesy of Michael Virtue, Virtue Books)

Right: Painting of the unprovoked attack on the United States Pacific Fleet at Pearl Harbor on 7 December 1941, by Montague B. Black. (Courtesy of Michael Virtue, Virtue Books)

AMERICAN INFLUENCE ON BRITISH CULTURE

Between 1942 and 1945, tens of thousands of young American servicemen, known as GIs, arrived in Britain. Their presence, despite spanning a very short period of time, would have a lasting effect on the communities they visited. By the end of the war almost 3 million GIs had passed through the country. By the time of D-Day, it is estimated that in Suffolk alone there was one GI for every six civilians.

After three years of war, what the Americans brought was a touch of glamour. They were far better paid than the British and wore much smarter uniforms. With most British men serving away in the forces, they were a great draw for the local women. Their camps put on dances and they seemed to have an endless supply of food, cigarettes, nylons, and other things which had been rationed here for some time. Many thousands of women became GI brides and after the war went to live in the United States. On the negative side, this period also resulted in thousands of unwanted pregnancies.

Adding to that sense of glamour, many famous Hollywood film stars and singers came to Britain to entertain the troops and nation. Personal appearances by people like Bob Hope, Bing Crosby and Jo Stafford all helped to boost morale. Then of course there was the swing music of people like Glen Miller and his band, along with vibrant dance styles, all of which helped to cheer people up.

One of the profoundest impacts of the American invasion was the British population coming into contact with so many black soldiers. In 1939 there were roughly 7,000 black people in Britain, but by D-Day there were 500,000 Afro-Americans. Because of this, many people would witness scenes of racial prejudice, and the system of segregation still prevalent in some parts of the USA at that time. The black and white troops lived in separate camps and did separate jobs. To avoid tension the two groups were permitted into the local towns on separate nights for socialising purposes.

So in terms of the American occupation of the British Isles during the Second World War, there were good and bad points, but without doubt the country's culture was irreversibly affected by their short stay.

Between 1942 and the end of the war, several thousand English girls married American GIs; many of them would later move to the States. (Courtesy of Sheila Petroff)

BATTLE OF HONG KONG

Among other simultaneous actions, while they attacked Pearl Harbor the Japanese were launching an assault against British-held Hong Kong. British and other Empire troops, including Indian forces, supported by the Hong Kong Volunteer Defence Forces, attempted to resist the rapidly advancing Japanese but were heavily outnumbered.

After racing down the New Territories and Kowloon, Japanese forces crossed Victoria Harbour on 18 December. After fierce fighting continued on Hong Kong Island, the only reservoir was lost. Canadian Winnipeg Grenadiers fought at the crucial Wong Nai Chong Gap that secured the passage between Hong Kong proper and secluded southern sections of the island. Finally defeated, on 25 December 1941, British colonial officials, headed by the Governor of Hong Kong, Mark Aitchison Young, surrendered at the Japanese headquarters. To the local people, the day was known as 'Black Christmas'.

Another significant British disaster at this time was the loss of two major warships, HMS *Repulse* and HMS *Prince of Wales*, which were sunk by a Japanese air attack off Malaya on 10 December 1941 and following the invasion of Thailand, the government of that country formally allied itself with Japan on 21 December.

5
1942: THE END OF THE BEGINNING

Now that the United States had entered the war, the Allies, while still trying to contain the Japanese in the East, could begin the process of defeating Germany in the West. Their first ambition was to defeat the Axis in North Africa, but ironically even before the Americans had entered the theatre, the British, with Commonwealth support, scored a resounding victory at El Alamein. Of the victory Winston Churchill was to say, 'Now this is not the end. It is not even the beginning of the end, but it is, perhaps, the end of the beginning.'

THE GRAND STRATEGY

In August 1941 Winston Churchill met with President Roosevelt, and even though America was not in the war at that time they began to discuss what would happen in the post-war period. Much of their discussions would form the basis of the Atlantic Charter. In the Declaration by United Nations of 1 January 1942, the Allies, including China, the Soviet Union and twenty-two other countries, many of which had exiled governments operating from Britain, affirmed the charter and took an obligation not to broker separate peace deals with the Axis powers.

During 1942 Allied officials debated on the appropriate grand strategy to pursue. All agreed that defeating Germany was the primary objective even though enough troops should be committed to the Far East in order to keep the Japanese checked.

The Americans favoured a straightforward, large-scale attack on Germany through France. The Soviets were demanding a second front from the east. But the British persuaded the Americans that a landing in France was unfeasible in 1942 and they should instead focus on driving the Axis out of North Africa.

BATTLE OF EL ALAMEIN

By January 1942, Commonwealth forces in North Africa had launched a counteroffensive known as Operation *Crusader* and reclaimed all the gains the Germans and Italians had made, but after receiving supplies and reinforcements from Tripoli, the Axis again attacked, defeating the Allies at Gazala in June and finally capturing Tobruk. The Axis forces then drove the British Eighth Army back over the Egyptian border, where their advance was stopped in July only 140 kilometres from Alexandria in the First Battle of El Alamein. After this and for the remainder of the campaign in North Africa, the Eighth Army would be commanded by Lieutenant General Bernard Montgomery.

The Axis forces under Field Marshal Erwin Rommel made a new attempt to break through to Cairo at the end of June but were pushed back. Then, after a period of building up and training, the British launched a major new offensive, in which they decisively defeated the German–Italian Army during the Second Battle of El Alamein in late October 1942.

The battle lasted from 23 October to 11 November and marked a major turning point in the war, ending the Axis threat to Egypt and the Suez Canal and

Boeing B-17 Flying Fortresses arrive in Britain from the United States ready for the bomber offensive against Nazi-held territory. (© Paul Chryst)

of gaining access to the Middle Eastern and Persian oilfields via North Africa. From a psychological perspective, the victory revived the morale of the Allies as it was the first major offensive against the Axis since the start of the European war in 1939 in which the Western Allies had achieved a decisive victory.

OPERATION *TORCH*

Operation *Torch* started on 8 November 1942 and finished on 11 November. In an attempt to pincer German and Italian forces, the Allies, made up of American, British and Commonwealth contingents, landed in Vichy-held French North Africa under the assumption that there would be little resistance. In reality the Vichy forces resolved to put up a strong defence in both Oran and Morocco, but not Algiers, where a *coup d'état* by the French resistance on 8 November succeeded in arresting the Vichy commanders and neutralising their army before the landing began. Consequently, the Allies met no opposition in Algiers and the city was captured on the first day. During the operation the Americans also fought a sea engagement with French and German ships, the naval Battle of Casablanca, which ended in a US victory.

After three days of subsequent talks and threats, generals Mark Clark and Dwight D. Eisenhower compelled Admiral Darlan to order the cessation of armed

German tanks moving across the French countryside. (Courtesy of the Amberley archives)

resistance in Oran and Morocco, with the proviso that Darlan would be head of a new Free French administration.

The Allied landings prompted the Axis occupation of Vichy France itself. In addition, the French fleet was captured at Toulon by the Italians, something which did them little good as the main portion of the fleet had been scuttled to prevent their use. The Vichy army in North Africa then joined the Allies and Free French Forces.

Following Operation *Torch* the Germans and Italians began to reinforce Tunisia with fresh troops to fill the vacuum left by Vichy soldiers, who had joined the Allies. During this period the Allies decided against a rapid advance into Tunisia while they wrestled with the Vichy authorities. However, by mid-November the Allies were able to advance into Tunisia but only in single-division strength. The Germans and Italians in the meantime, with their reinforcements, stopped the Allied advance thirty kilometres from Tunis and then began to push them back.

THE SIEGE OF MALTA

The British island of Malta was under siege from 1940 to 1942. Its position in the Mediterranean made it strategically important to both sides. For the British, the campaign in North Africa increased the island's considerable value. From here British air and sea forces based on the island could attack Axis ships transporting vital supplies and reinforcements from Europe.

The Axis resolved to bomb or starve Malta into submission by attacking its ports, towns and cities, and by targeting ships that supplied it. Malta was one of the most intensively bombed areas during the war. The German and Italian air forces flew a total of 3,000 bombing raids over a period of two years in an effort to destroy RAF defences and the ports. Success in this would have made it possible for the Axis to land troops on the island, but this did not happen, and the Allied convoys continued to supply and reinforce the island. The siege effectively ended in November 1942, and, as witness to the heroism and devotion of the people of Malta, King George VI famously awarded the entire island the George Cross.

THE DIEPPE RAID

While all of this had been going on, back in Europe Allied commandos had been carrying out raids on strategic targets, which culminated in the disastrous raid on the town of Dieppe known as Operation *Jubilee* on 19 August 1942, when a force of mainly Canadian troops landed on the north coast of France.

Among the objectives of *Jubilee* was to test the feasibility of seizing and holding a major port, both to prove it was possible and to gather intelligence from captured prisoners. If successful it would boost morale in Britain, as well as assuring the Soviet Union and the French Resistance that the Allies were committed to opening a second front in Western Europe.

It was only ever intended to be a raid, and with all objectives achieved the troops would evacuate the beaches and return to England after twenty-four hours. However, from the start it was a disaster.

The assault began at 5 a.m., but by 10.50 a.m. the Allied commanders were forced to order the retreat. Of the 6,086 men who actually made it ashore 3,623 had been killed, wounded or captured.

Among the Royal Navy's losses were thirty-three landing craft and 550 personnel dead or injured. The RAF lost ninety-six aircraft and sixty-two aircrew were killed – although, as with all wartime engagements, these figures remain debated.

SUMMER OFFENSIVE ON THE EASTERN FRONT

Despite considerable losses, in early 1942 Germany and its allies stopped a major Soviet offensive in central and southern Russia, keeping most territorial gains they had achieved during the previous year. In May the Germans defeated the Soviets in the Kerch Peninsula and at Kharkiv, and then launched their main summer offensive against southern Russia in June, to seize the oilfields of the Caucasus and occupy the Kuban steppe, while maintaining positions on the northern and central areas of the front.

The Soviets decided to make a stand at Stalingrad, which was in the path of the advancing German armies. By mid-November, the Germans had nearly captured the city, street by street against stiff resistance. But then the Soviets began their second winter counteroffensive, starting with an encirclement of the German forces at Stalingrad and an unsuccessful attack on the Rzhev salient near Moscow, where they suffered huge casualties.

JAPANESE ADVANCE IN THE PACIFIC

The Japanese began 1942 by capturing Manila and the Cavite naval base in the Philippines, forcing American and Filipino troops to retreat into the jungles of Bataan. They also advanced into Borneo and on 11 January captured Kuala

Lumpur in Malaya. But these are just a few of Japan's successes at this time – they attacked and invaded Allied possessions all over the South Pacific.

On 9 April Major-General Edward King surrendered Bataan against the orders of General Douglas MacArthur. Some 78,000 troops, of which 66,000 were Filipinos and 12,000 Americans, were taken captive. This was the largest contingent of US soldiers ever to surrender.

The prisoners were at once led to the southern end of the Bataan peninsula on what became known as the 'Bataan Death March.' At least 600 Americans and 5,000 Filipinos died because of the extreme brutality of their captors, who starved, beat, and kicked them on the way; those who became too weak to walk were bayoneted. Those who survived were eventually placed in POW camps.

By the end of April, Japan and its ally Thailand had almost fully conquered Burma, Malaya, the Dutch East Indies, Singapore, and Rabaul in Australian New Guinea, inflicting severe losses on Allied troops and taking a large number of prisoners.

Despite stubborn resistance at Corregidor, the part of the Philippines in US possession was eventually captured in May, forcing its government into exile. Japanese forces also achieved naval victories in the South China Sea, Java Sea and Indian Ocean and bombed the Allied naval base at Darwin, Australia. The only real Allied success against Japan was a Chinese victory at Changsha in early January. These victories, however, made the Japanese overconfident, as well as overextended.

Men of the Burma Rifles preparing to defend their homeland against the Japanese. (Courtesy of Michael Virtue, Virtue Books)

THE PACIFIC TIDE BEGINS TO TURN

In early May Japan initiated operations to capture Port Moresby in New Guinea by amphibious assault and thus sever communications and supply lines between the United States and Australia. The Allies, however, prevented the invasion by intercepting and defeating the Japanese naval forces in the Battle of the Coral Sea.

Japan's next plan was to seize the Midway Atoll and lure American carriers into battle to be eliminated. As a diversion, Japan would also send forces to occupy the Aleutian Islands in Alaska. In early June, Japan put its operations into action but the Americans, having broken Japanese naval codes in late May, were fully aware of the plans and used this knowledge to achieve a decisive victory at Midway over the Imperial Japanese Navy.

With its capacity greatly diminished as a result of the Midway battle, Japan chose to focus on a belated attempt to capture Port Moresby by marching overland. The Americans planned a counter-attack against Japanese positions in the southern Solomon Islands, primarily Guadalcanal, as a first step towards capturing Rabaul, which was now the main Japanese base in South East Asia.

Both plans started in July, but by mid-September, the Battle of Guadalcanal took priority for the Japanese, and troops in New Guinea were ordered to withdraw from the Port Moresby area to the northern part of the island, where they faced Australian and United States troops in the Battle of Buna-Gona. Guadalcanal soon became a focal point for both sides with heavy commitments of troops and ships.

During the naval Battle of Midway the Japanese Navy suffered a crippling defeat. Here we see the aircraft carrier USS *Hornet*, which played a vital role that day. (Courtesy of Michael Virtue, Virtue Books)

6

1943: THE BEGINNING OF THE END

If 1942 had been the end of the beginning, 1943 was certainly the beginning of the end for the Axis forces. With the Allies successfully invading mainland Europe through Sicily and mainland Italy, and the Soviets defeating the Germans at Stalingrad, it was only a matter of time for Hitler and Mussolini, while in the Far East, operations against the Japanese were also going to plan.

CASABLANCA CONFERENCE

After Rommel's defeat at El Alamein and other Allied victories in North Africa, President Roosevelt met with Winston Churchill in Morocco for the Casablanca Conference, from 14 to 24 January 1943. The most notable developments at the conference were the finalisation of Allied strategic plans and the absolute insistence on the unconditional surrender of Germany.

In order to secure the Mediterranean supply routes it was also agreed that an initial invasion of Europe should be made through Sicily and mainland Italy in 1943, with a full-scale assault on the Atlantic coast of France in 1944.

BATTLE OF KASSERINE PASS

During the winter of 1942/43, there followed a period of stalemate in North Africa during which time both sides continued to build up their forces, but in the second half of February, in eastern Tunisia, Rommel and Hans-Jürgen von Arnim, the German commander in Tunisia, had some successes against the mainly inexperienced French and Americans, most notably in routing the latter at the Battle of Kasserine Pass.

Fighting around the Kasserine Pass began in December 1942 when the Germans attempted to link their two armies. Von Arnim wanted to control the Eastern Dorsale of the Atlas Mountains to the south of Tunis and, if successful, to push

Eisenhower's troops further south, through the Kasserine Pass. This would isolate them from their supply lines and allow von Arnim to link up with Rommel.

On 3 January the Germans began to attack French troops, which Eisenhower decided to withdraw and replace with fresh American soldiers newly arrived. However, by the end of January the Germans had secured a bridgehead in Tunisia, giving Rommel a safe enclave to move into. Then on 14 February the Germans attacked again under cover of a sandstorm. They quickly destroyed forty-four American tanks as well as a considerable amount of artillery and other vehicles.

The following day the Americans launched a counter-attack, but by the 17th they had lost a further ninety-eight tanks, fifty-seven halftracks and twenty-nine artillery pieces. As they withdrew, the Americans destroyed vital supplies to keep them out of enemy hands; however, the Germans did manage to capture 5,000 gallons of aviation fuel.

British infantry attack Longstop Hill in Tunisia, backed by Churchill tanks of the North Irish Horse. (© Henry Buckton)

RATIONING

Because of the German U-boat threat, not long after the start of the war a system for rationing food was put in place as it was becoming more and more difficult to get supplies into British ports from other parts of the world. Therefore the food that the nation consumed over the next few years would have to be almost entirely homegrown. To make sure that everybody had an equal share of essential foodstuffs and in order that shopkeepers did not benefit from these shortages by raising prices, each person was limited to a restricted amount.

National Registration Day was 29 September 1939, and every householder in the country was required to complete a form listing all those who lived at their address. From this data the government issued everyone with their identity card and a ration book containing coupons. Then, from 8 January 1940, each time somebody wished to purchase a rationed item they were required to hand their book to the retailer together with the money, and the retailer would then cut out the necessary coupon.

A typical weekly supply of groceries was limited to four ounces of ham or bacon; two ounces of cheese; eight ounces of sugar; eight ounces of butter, margarine or lard; three pints of milk; two ounces of tea; four ounces of sweets; and one fresh egg per person. They could also have meat, other than bacon or ham, to the value of one shilling and twopence, which roughly amounted to four sausages and one pork chop. Not everything was rationed, and locally grown seasonal fruit and vegetables could be consumed at will. Of course this was slightly unfair on people living in cities as these items were not as easily obtainable as they were for those living in the country.

As well as food, many other things became very scarce during the war simply because most industry had been dedicated to providing things for the war effort, and other rationed items included petrol and clothing.

Above: Digging for victory: the queen visits an evacuation school in Horsted Keynes, where a boy from Battersea prepares ground for food crops. (Courtesy of Michael Virtue, Virtue Books)

Below left: A member of the Women's Land Army working on a tractor. (Courtesy of Michael Virtue, Virtue books)

Below right: A National Registration Identity Card carried by all UK citizens. (Author's collection)

THE WOMEN'S LAND ARMY

During the Second World War, many young men who had worked in farming before the war were called into the armed forces and were therefore unable to help produce the food the nation required. Also, because of German attacks on Allied merchant vessels, it was difficult to obtain supplies from abroad. It was therefore decided that the women of Britain should help to produce what was needed. The Women's Land Army (WLA) was a British civilian organisation created during both world wars as the answer to this problem. Women who worked for the WLA were commonly known as Land Girls, and there was a similar organuisation founded in the United States of America at the same time.

Although the WLA had existed in the First World War, it was reinstigated by the government in June 1939, as by then war was deemed almost inevitable. The vast majority of the Land Girls already lived in the countryside so were accustomed to the lifestyle, but more than a third came from London and the industrial cities of the north of England, so for them it came as a big shock. Previously they might have worked a nine-to-five life in an office or factory, if they worked at all. Now they were required to be up at the crack of dawn to milk cows, plough fields and gather crops.

In the Second World War, the WLA came under the auspices of the Ministry of Agriculture and Fisheries and their honorary head was Lady Denman. At first it asked for volunteers, but they were later supplemented by conscripts as the situation became more severe. By 1944 the WLA had over 80,000 members working in farms of varying sizes and types all over the country, and operating some of the most sophisticated equipment of the day. It was a time of great change in agriculture and the Land Girls would have been equally competent working with horses or tractors after training. The WLA lasted until its official disbandment on 21 October 1949, and there is no doubt that their effort in feeding troops and civilians alike was a vital factor in winning the war.

FINAL VICTORY IN NORTH AFRICA

Encouraged by their success at Kasserine, German High Command ordered Rommel to attack the Allies at Le Kef, which was some sixty miles north of the pass, through which he would have to lead his men in order to achieve the task. The field marshal was unhappy with this as many of his soldiers had been withdrawn to fight on the Eastern Front. Also, he had serious problems with supplies. Because of this he called the attack off on 22 February and quietly slipped away. So by the end of February the Kasserine Pass was back in Allied hands.

By the beginning of March, the British Eighth Army, advancing westward along the North African coast from Egypt, finally reached the Tunisian border in pursuit of Rommel, who found himself in a two-army pincer with the British to the east and the Americans to the west. The Germans were outflanked and outgunned and on 13 May they had little choice but to surrender, yielding over 275,000 prisoners of war. Shortly afterwards all Italian colonies in Africa had been captured.

German soldiers who surrendered to the British in North Africa. (Courtesy of Michael Virtue, Virtue Books)

SURRENDER OF GERMAN ARMY AT STALINGRAD

The Battle of Stalingrad had begun in the summer of 1942. Yet despite repeated attempts, the Germans under Friedrich von Paulus could not break the determined resistance of the Soviet Army, even though they were almost entirely surrounded.

Diminishing resources, partisan guerrilla attacks and the cruelty of the Russian winter began to take their toll on the Germans. Then, on 19 November, the Soviets made their move, launching a counteroffensive that began with a massive artillery bombardment. The Soviets then encircled the enemy and launched attacks from the north and south simultaneously, overrunning the defences all along the line until surrender was their only option. But Hitler wouldn't hear of it: 'The Sixth Army will hold its positions to the last man and the last round,' he insisted. Von Paulus held out until 31 January, when he finally succumbed. Of his original army of 280,000 men, the remaining 91,000 were taken prisoner.

BATTLE FOR KURSK

After the defeat at Stalingrad the remaining German forces on the eastern front spent the spring and early summer of 1943 making preparations for a large-scale offensive in central Russia. On 4 July they attacked the Soviets around the Kursk Bulge, but within a week had exhausted themselves against the defenders. For the first time in the war, Hitler cancelled the operation before it had achieved tactical or operational success. His decision was partially due to events far away in Sicily where the Western Allies had started an invasion.

The Soviet victory at Kursk brought to an end Germany's hopes of winning the eastern war and gaining lands for its people to colonise, and although they attempted to stabilise the front along the hastily fortified Panther–Wotan line, the Soviets had soon broken through at Smolensk and elsewhere. Hitler's dream for Lebensraum was all but over.

COMBINED BOMBER OFFENSIVE OVER GERMANY

In early 1943 the British and Americans began the Combined Bomber Offensive, a strategic bombing campaign against Germany. The goals were to disrupt the German war economy, reduce morale, and 'de-house' the civilian population. By the end of the war most German cities would be reduced to rubble and 7.5 million people made homeless.

The British bombing campaign was chiefly waged by night with large numbers of heavy bombers until the latter stages of the war, when German fighter defences were so reduced that daylight bombing was possible without risking large losses. The US effort was by day with massed formations of bombers escorted by fighter aircraft. Together they made up a round-the-clock bombing effort, except where weather conditions prevented operations.

Operation *Pointblank* was the code name for the primary portion of the Allied Combined Bomber Offensive intended to cripple or destroy the German aircraft fighter strength, thus drawing it away from frontline operations and ensuring it would not be an obstacle to the invasion of north-west Europe. The *Pointblank* directive of 14 June ordered RAF Bomber Command and the US Eighth Air Force to bomb specific targets such as aircraft factories.

Up to a point the bombing was aimed at German industry, but its secondary task was to destroy large areas of human habitation. This was particularly effective in July 1943 when the British firebombed Hamburg during Operation *Gomorrah*. The attacks created one of the largest firestorms of the entire war, killing 42,600 civilians and wounding 37,000 more and practically destroying the entire city. But this was merely a taste of the fate in store for other German cities in the months ahead.

INVASION OF SICILY

On the night of 9 July 1943, Operation *Husky*, the invasion of Sicily, got underway. The Americans landed on the beaches of the Gulf of Gela, while the British, Commonwealth and Canadian forces landed at the south-eastern tip of Sicily, around Pachino and the Gulf of Noto.

High winds made the landings extremely difficult, especially for the paratroopers, who were dropped in to create a little confusion before the amphibious assault began. Some of the British-led troops moved north-west across the Hyblaean Mountains, while others went north to capture Syracuse.

The Americans, meanwhile, came up against greater resistance as they were met by one of the two German battalions on the island. After securing their beachheads, however, they headed westward towards Agrigento and then across the centre to Palermo.

There was some confusion after the successful landing as to who would be doing what. Plans had been laid for the initial attack but beyond that the rest of the campaign was somewhat improvised. The ground forces commander, General

Above: An American bomber crew in England in 1943, on the way to board their aircraft before a mission over the Continent. (© Paul Chryst)

Below: This atmospheric photograph of a gunner keeping his eyes peeled for enemy aircraft was taken inside a B-17 during a mission over the Continent. (© Paul Chryst)

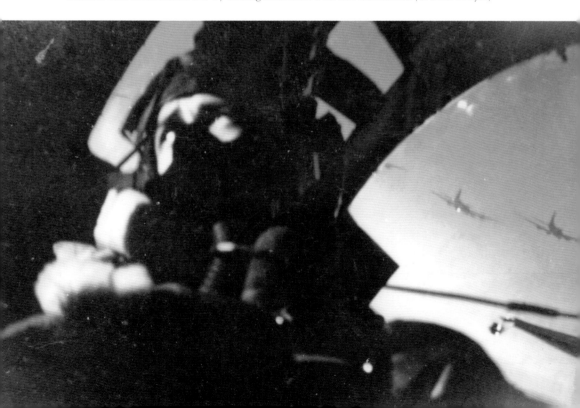

Sir Harold Alexander, and the commander of the American forces, General Patton, seemed to distrust each other, and the latter began to disobey the former, eager to demonstrate the superiority of the American Army.

Patton marched his men to Palermo despite being instructed to head further west. However, Sicily's capital fell easily, and almost immediately the sensational news erupted that Mussolini and his fascist government had been overthrown.

With Italian forces on the island in total disarray, both Allied armies began to march on Messina. The Americans arrived first on 17 August, as the British-led forces had faced the difficult task of getting around Catania and Mount Etna, where stubborn German forces had dug in. By this time, however, over 100,000 German and Italian troops, as well as large quantities of military equipment, had been successfully transferred to the Italian mainland. The significance of this was the fact that the fight up the Italian peninsula would be considerably more difficult than hoped for.

The invasion of Sicily was preceded by a month-long air bombardment of Axis air bases. This painting by S. Drigin shows an attack on the airfield at Catania. (Courtesy of Michael Virtue, Virtue Books)

INVASION OF MAINLAND ITALY

On 3 September the Allies began the invasion of the Italian mainland, with Montgomery's British-led army landing at the toe of Italy after an extensive artillery bombardment and the Americans landing at Salerno near Naples on 9 September. Just before the assault commenced the new Italian government, which had replaced Mussolini's regime, surrendered, and ordered Italians not to resist.

Consequently the southern part of the country was conquered very quickly, including several crucial facilities such as the Foggia airfield, which the United States Air Force and the RAF would employ as a bomber base against the Nazis. They also secured the port of Naples, which was vital as a supply artery. Germany responded by disarming Italian forces, seizing military control of Italian areas, and creating a series of defensive lines across the country. German Special Forces then rescued Mussolini, who established a new client state in German-occupied Italy named the Italian Social Republic, causing an Italian civil war.

By mid-November the Allies had reached the Gustav Line, which comprised natural and manmade fortifications to the south of Rome. Here the Germans dug in with fresh reinforcements arriving.

BATTLE OF THE ATLANTIC

It is difficult to place the Battle of the Atlantic on to a chronological timeline of the Second World War as it was ongoing for much of the conflict, but in 1943 it certainly came to a head. At its core was the Allied naval blockade of Germany and Germany's subsequent counter-blockade. It was at its height from mid-1940 through to the end of 1943. The battle pitted U-boats and other warships of the German Navy and aircraft of the German Air Force against the Royal Navy, Royal Canadian Navy, and Allied merchant shipping. The convoys, coming mainly from North America and predominantly going to the United Kingdom and the Soviet Union, were protected for the most part by the British and Canadians. These forces were later aided by ships and aircraft of the United States when that nation entered the war, while the Germans were joined by submarines of the Italian Royal Navy after Italy joined the fray.

As an island nation, the United Kingdom was highly dependent on imported goods. Britain required more than a million tons of imported material per week in order to be able to survive and fight. In essence, the Battle of the Atlantic was a tonnage war: the Allied struggle to supply Britain and the Axis attempt to stem the flow of merchant shipping that enabled Britain to keep fighting.

From 1942 onwards, the Germans also sought to prevent the build-up of Allied supplies and equipment in the British Isles in preparation for the invasion of occupied Europe.

The outcome of the battle was a strategic victory for the Allies but at great cost: 3,500 merchant ships and 175 warships were sunk for the loss of 783 U-boats.

ENIGMA CODEBREAKERS

An important part of the Allied victory in the Battle of the Atlantic was played by the British Government Code and Cypher School at Bletchley Park. The U-boat campaign required large volumes of communications between the boats and their headquarters. This was thought to be safe as the radio messages were enciphered using the Enigma cipher machine, which the Germans considered unbreakable.

At the start of the battle it was generally believed by the codebreakers at Bletchley that Enigma could not be broken. But if they were to crack the codes the British needed to get their hands on German equipment. This was provided by the Royal Navy after they captured a number of enemy submarines. Material

British sailors with a captured German U-boat, from which equipment was extracted that was vital to the codebreakers at Bletchley Park. (Courtesy of Michael Virtue, Virtue Books)

extracted from these U-boats allowed all U-boat traffic to be read for several weeks and the familiarity the codebreakers gained with the unusual content of messages helped in breaking the codes.

Once the British had learned how to translate the codes it enabled them to plot the positions of U-boat patrol lines and route convoys around them. Because of this merchant shipping losses dropped by over two-thirds and more supplies were able to get through.

ALLIES GAIN MOMENTUM IN THE FAR EAST

In 1943, although the Allied emphasis was on defeating Germany, the strategy for the Far East was also taking shape. In November President Roosevelt and Winston Churchill met with Chiang Kai-shek in Cairo and then with Joseph Stalin in Tehran. The former conference determined the post-war return of Japanese territory, while the latter included a commitment that the Western Allies would invade France in 1944 and that the Soviet Union would declare war on Japan within three months of Germany's defeat.

By the start of 1943, the Japanese had been defeated on the island of Guadalcanal, while in Burma, Commonwealth forces mounted two operations. The first, an offensive into the Arakan region in late 1942, was a disaster and ended in a retreat back to India by May. The second was the insertion of irregular forces behind Japanese lines from February onwards which, by the end of April, had achieved dubious results.

In May Allied forces were sent to clear the Japanese out of the Aleutian Islands, and soon after began major operations to isolate Rabaul by capturing the surrounding territories. They also began to breach the Japanese central Pacific perimeter at the Gilbert and Marshall Islands.

While all of this was taking place, the Chinese were forcing their occupiers to fight a costly war of attrition in the Battle of Changde, in the Hunan province of China. So on all fronts, 1943 was ending with the Allies in the ascendency.

7

1944: THE INVASION OF WESTERN EUROPE BEGINS

1944 was the year of Operation *Overlord*, which marked one of the most important days in modern history. After building up a huge reserve of men and equipment in Britain in what was code named Operation *Bolero*, the American Army set about training for the amphibious assault on the coast of France. This took place largely in the west of the country in counties like Devon and Cornwall, while the British and Canadians mainly trained in the east of the country beyond Portsmouth. But while these soldiers prepared at home for the greatest seaborne invasion of all time, elsewhere Allied soldiers were still engaged in desperate fighting.

MONTE CASSINO AND THE ANZIO LANDINGS

At the beginning of 1944 in Italy, the Germans were dug in to the south of Rome along the Gustav Line. The area was dominated by Monte Cassino, a historic hilltop abbey which looked out across the entrances to the Liri and Rapido valleys, along which the Allies would have to advance. Here, the Germans were heavily defending the surrounding mountainside. In order to capture Rome the Allies would have to take Monte Cassino, and on 17 January they launched the first in a series of attacks.

At the same time, in an attempt to outflank the Germans and in so doing attack Rome without having to pass Monte Cassino, the Allies also made a seaborne landing at Anzio called Operation *Shingle* on 22 January. The operation was commanded by the American major general John Lucas and the initial landings achieved complete surprise. However, instead of taking advantage of their good fortune and moving straight on to the capital, Lucas decided to take his time and entrenched his troops against a possible counter-attack. This gave Field Marshal Albert Kesselring, the German commander in Italy, time to move every spare unit he could into a ring around the beachhead. Here his gunners had a clear view of every Allied position and were able to rain shells down on to them.

Meanwhile, back at Cassino the Allies bombed the abbey on 15 February, fearing that the Germans had been using it for defensive purposes. American aircraft proceeded to drop 1,400 tons of bombs, leaving the abbey in ruins. But ironically, the rubble provided the Germans with better protection from aerial and artillery attacks, so two days later, German paratroopers took up positions in the abbey's ruins. Between 17 January and 18 May, Monte Cassino and the Gustav defences were assaulted four times before the German defenders were finally driven off.

At Anzio, Lucas was relieved of his command to be replaced by General Lucian Truscott and the Allies finally broke out of the beachhead in May. Rome was captured on 4 June but unfortunately many of the German defenders both from Anzio and the Gustav Line were able to withdraw and regroup to the north of Rome to hold their next defensive position, the Gothic Line.

A painting that shows the effect of the Allied bombing on the monastery at Monte Cassino, on 15 February 1944. (© Henry Buckton)

THE SIEGE OF LENINGRAD IS LIFTED

At the end of January the siege of Leningrad was finally lifted following a major Soviet offensive. The siege had started on 8 September 1941, when the Germans had severed the last road in to the city, and ended on 27 January 1944. It was one of the longest and most destructive sieges in history and without question the most lethal in terms of casualties, which resulted in the deaths of up to 1.5 million soldiers and civilians.

The German Army in the east was now in retreat and although the Soviets were held for a while on the pre-war Estonian border by a combined German and Estonian force, the latter fighting to re-establish national independence, by late May the Russians had liberated the Crimea and largely expelled Axis forces from Ukraine and made incursions into Romania.

HELSINKI AND THE GREAT RAIDS

In February the Soviet Union launched three massive bombing raids against Helsinki in Finland known as the Great Raids. The aim was to break the Finnish fighting spirit and force the Finns to the peace table. The raids were conducted on the nights of 6–7, 16–17 and 26–27 February. Joseph Stalin had obtained British and American support for this measure at the Tehran Conference in 1943. In this manner the USSR hoped to force Finland to break its ties with Germany and agree to a peace settlement.

ARP workers of Helsinki searching the ruins of a bomb-shattered building during the Great Raids. (Courtesy of Michael Virtue, Virtue Books)

THE BLACKOUT

At night, all large cities and towns generate a tremendous amount of light. If the Germans wanted to bomb civilian centres or factories in the dark hours, all they had to do was head for this light source. So in order to minimise the danger, all homes and businesses were ordered to 'black out'. In private houses this meant spending much of your time in darkness, as all windows and doors had to be covered with something dark, such as curtains or wooden boards, to prevent any light escaping. People also protected their windows against the effects of the blasts of bombs dropped nearby. One way of doing this was to stick strips of brown paper across the windowpanes. But even after all these precautions had been implemented, the use of lights or open fires was kept to a minimum in order to prevent an ARP warden from banging on your door ordering you to 'Put that light out!'

Even away from the cities and towns the blackout had to be observed. If enemy aircraft failed to locate their target, they were likely to drop their bombs on any light source they observed emanating from below. Also, the entire country was covered in sites supporting the war effort in some way. These sites could have been in very rural locations, so the twinkling lights of a nearby village or farm might have been all the German navigators required to locate them.

During the war all street lights were turned off, so in an attempt to avoid accidents in the dark, lamp posts were painted with white stripes, as were the sides of kerbs. Travelling by motor transport at night was to be avoided unless absolutely necessary, in which case the headlights on cars had to have special shields over them, so that only a small amount of light pointed down towards the ground. Buses had a similar arrangement: their lights were covered and a small beam of light from a hole was all the driver had to light his way. People began to wear fluorescent armbands and strips on their clothing, and while batteries were still available they were allowed to carry torches but, similarly to the buses, had to cover the light, leaving just a tiny pinhole to see by.

"We'll give her another ten minutes, and then warn her."

A humorous look at ARP wardens enforcing the blackout. (Author's collection)

It is thought that 2,121 bombers were employed in the three raids, and more than 16,000 bombs were dropped. The Finns deceived Soviet pathfinders by lighting fires on the islands outside the city, and only using the searchlights to the east of it, thereby making the enemy crews think the city was elsewhere. Because of this only 530 bombs fell on the capital itself and consequently the casualties were quite low compared to other places bombed during the war.

German Troops Occupy Hungary

Although Hungary had been part of the Axis with Germany, in early 1944 it began to discuss an armistice with the Allies. On discovering this Hitler implemented Operation *Margarethe* and on 12 March his troops began to seize Hungarian facilities.

FW 190 fighter bombers of the German Air Force on an airfield somewhere on the Eastern Front. (© Paul Chryst)

As a ruse to get him out of the country, Hitler invited the Hungarian regent Miklos Horthy to the palace of Klessheim near Salzburg for negotiations, and while he was there German forces quietly moved into Hungary. When Horthy returned to Budapest he was met by German soldiers at the train station. He was then informed that Hungary could only remain sovereign if he removed his prime minister in favour of a government that would cooperate fully with the Nazis. The occupation was a complete surprise and therefore quick and bloodless.

COUNTERMEASURES IN ASIA

At the start of 1944 the Allies experienced mixed fortunes in mainland Asia. In March the Japanese launched the first of two invasions, which was an operation against British positions in Assam. This led to the siege of Commonwealth troops at Imphal and Kohima. In May British forces mounted a counteroffensive that drove Japanese troops back to Burma. At the same time Chinese forces that had invaded northern Burma in late 1943 besieged Japanese troops in Myitkyina.

The second Japanese invasion attempted to destroy China's main fighting forces, secure railways between Japanese-held areas and capture Allied airfields. By June, the Japanese had conquered the province of Henan and begun a renewed attack against Changsha in the Hunan province.

The Japanese Prime Minister Hideki Tojo, who was forced to resign after his country's defeat in the Battle of the Philippine Sea. (Courtesy of Michael Virtue, Virtue Books)

By the end of March the Allies had eliminated Japanese forces from the Aleutians and additionally neutralised the major Japanese base at Truk Lagoon in the Caroline Islands. In April, the Allies then launched an operation to retake western New Guinea. On 15 June US troops made an amphibious assault on the Japanese-held island of Saipan in the Mariana Islands; the defending troops surrendered on 7 July. On 19 June the US Navy defeated the Japanese in a massive air battle known as the Battle of the Philippine Sea, during which the Japanese lost more than 400 aircraft and three aircraft carriers.

OPERATION OVERLORD

Operation *Overlord* was the codename given to the Allied invasion of France scheduled for June 1944. The overall commander was General Dwight D. Eisenhower. Other senior commanders included Air Marshall Leigh-Mallory, Air Marshall Tedder, General Bernard Montgomery and Admiral Bertram Ramsey.

The planning and logistics behind *Overlord* were unparalleled in history. The Allies had to ensure that none of the plan was released, and above all the

Above: The ground crew of a B-17 at Bassingbourn in England prepare their aircraft ahead of the invasion of Europe. (© Paul Chryst)

Below: It's the day before D-Day, and landing craft are being loaded at the quiet fishing port of Brixham in Devon before the greatest seaborne invasion in history. (Courtesy of Alan Heather, Torquay Museum)

deception implemented to fool the Germans into thinking that the Pas-de-Calais was the main target, not Normandy.

The gathering of the equipment needed for the invasion was an enormous problem in itself. Where could it be stored without attracting the attention of enemy spies? How could it be transported to selected places in the south without local people talking about it? How could the thousands of boats needed for the invasion be gathered and readied? The plan also included the movement of two artificial harbours known as the Mulberrries, so that men and materials could be landed with more ease once the landing beaches had been secured. These were made up of huge concrete caissons that were sunk off the coast of Sussex to hide them from view and then refloated and towed across the Channel when required.

THE NORMANDY LANDINGS

Operation *Neptune* was the code name for the landing operations on D-Day itself, which took place on Tuesday 6 June 1944. The operation, planned by a team under Lieutenant General Sir Frederick Morgan, was the largest amphibious invasion in world history and was executed by land, sea and air.

The landings took place along an eighty-kilometre stretch of the Normandy coast divided into five sectors. The British landed on Sword Beach and Gold Beach, the Canadians on Juno Beach, and the Americans on Omaha Beach and Utah Beach. Prior to the seaborne landings, soldiers from three airborne divisions descended by parachute and glider on the flanks of the invasion area. The American 82nd and 101st Airborne Divisions were dropped into a zone at the base of the Cotentin Peninsula, and secured their objectives. The British 6th Airborne Division at the eastern end captured key bridges over the Caen Canal and Orne River, perhaps the most famous being Pegasus Bridge.

When the seaborne units began to land about 6.30 a.m. the Allied soldiers stormed the beaches against fierce opposition from German gunners and mined beach obstacles. The soldiers raced across the wide, open beaches that were being swept with machine-gun fire, and stormed the defences. Then, in fierce hand-to-hand fighting, they fought their way into the towns and hills and advanced inland.

By the end of the day the 3rd British Division was within three miles of Caen, the 3rd Canadian Division was well established on its intermediate objectives and the 50th Division was only two miles from Bayeux. In the American zone, the

HM the King inspects British airborne troops during an exercise in England. (Courtesy of Michael Virtue, Virtue Books)

4th Division had established a four-mile-deep penetration inland and was within reach of Sainte-Mère-Église, where the 82nd had fought throughout the night. The assault forces at Omaha Beach had met fierce resistance, incurring significant casualties, but here too beachheads had been established.

It was a magnificent accomplishment; the formidable Atlantic Wall had been successfully breached. By the end of D-Day, the Allies had landed more than 150,000 troops in France by sea and air, 6,000 vehicles including 900 tanks, 600 artillery pieces and about 4,000 tons of supplies. Amazingly, this had all been achieved with complete surprise.

GERMANY'S TERROR WEAPONS

On 13 June, while the fighting in Normandy intensified, the Nazis fired the first V-1 flying bomb against Britain. This was the first of Hitler's terror weapons to be launched against London and other cities in southern Britain. In total, 9,521 'doodlebugs', as they became known, were fired at Britain before the Allies overran their launch sites in October. This caused the remaining V-1s to be directed at the port of Antwerp and other targets in Belgium, with a further 2,448 being launched until their sites were also overrun, the last on 29 March 1945.

By the end of the war, as well as the V-1 and V-2 terror weapons, Germany also had the Messerschmitt Me 262, the world's first operational jet aircraft. (© Paul Chryst)

The V-2 rocket, on the other hand, was the world's first long-range ballistic missile and the first known human object to enter outer space. Beginning in September 1944, over 3,000 V-2s were launched against Allied targets, principally London and later Antwerp and Liège.

THE SOVIET ADVANCE

On 22 June, the Soviets launched an offensive in Belarus followed shortly afterwards by successful pushes in western Ukraine and eastern Poland, the latter of which prompted resistance fighters to initiate several uprisings, though the largest of these, in Warsaw, as well as a Slovak uprising in the south, were quashed by the Germans.

In eastern Romania the Red Army cut off and destroyed enemy troops still holding out there, which triggered successful uprisings in Romania and Bulgaria. Both of these countries then shifted their allegiance to the Allies.

In Yugoslavia, communist-led partisans under Marshal Tito had been fighting a guerrilla war since the start of the occupation in 1941, but in September 1944 the Soviets invaded the country, forcing the rapid withdrawal of the remaining German forces there. This was followed by the surrender of Axis forces in Greece on 4 November and in Albania on 29 November.

Soviet infantrymen advancing into western Ukraine in June 1944. (Courtesy of Michael Virtue, Virtue Books)

In northern Serbia, the Red Army, with limited support from Bulgarian forces, assisted the partisans in a joint liberation of the capital city of Belgrade on 20 October. A few days later, the Soviets launched a massive assault against German-occupied Hungary that lasted until the fall of Budapest in February 1945.

In contrast with impressive Soviet victories in the Balkans, the bitter Finnish resistance to the Soviet offensive in the Karelian Isthmus denied them occupation of Finland and led to the signing of a Soviet–Finnish armistice on relatively mild terms. Afterwards there was a subsequent shift to the Allied side by Finland.

The first city within Germany itself to be captured by the Allies was Aachen, which fell to the Americans on 21 October after a long battle. This success was quickly followed by the invasion of eastern Prussia by Soviet troops and the fall of Strasbourg on 24 November. Strasbourg had been annexed into Germany by the Nazis in 1940, who claimed it was a German city. It is now back in France again.

CLOSING IN ON JAPAN

By the start of July, Commonwealth forces in South East Asia had repelled the Japanese sieges in Assam, pushing the Japanese back to the Chindwin River while the Chinese captured Myitkyina. But in China itself, the Japanese were still having some success. They finally captured Changsha in mid-June and the city of Hengyang by early August. Soon after, they further invaded the province of Guangxi, winning major engagements against Chinese forces at Guilin and Liuzhou by the end of November and successfully linking up their forces in China and Indochina by the middle of December.

The American victory in the Battle of the Philippine Sea had forced the resignation of the Japanese Prime Minister, Hideki Tojo, and provided the United States with air bases from which to launch intensive heavy bomber attacks on the Japanese home islands. On 20 July the US made an amphibious assault on the island of Guam, which they had completely recaptured by 10 August. They also assaulted the island of Tinian on 24 July.

In late October, American forces invaded the Filipino island of Leyte, and shortly afterwards Allied naval forces scored another large victory during the Battle of Leyte Gulf, one of the largest naval battles in history. On 24 November American B-29 bombers began a massive bombing campaign against mainland Japan.

Operation Dragoon

Since the successful invasion of Normandy the Allies had made rapid advances. Caen was liberated on 9 July, while in Italy Florence fell on 4 August. On 20 July German military leaders attempted but failed to kill Adolf Hitler in the Rastenburg Assassination Plot. Hitler retaliated by killing 200 suspected plotters.

On 15 August the Allies launched Operation *Dragoon*, the invasion of southern France. It started with a parachute drop by the 1st Airborne Task Force, followed by an amphibious assault by elements of the US Army, reinforced by the French First Army. The landing caused the Germans to abandon southern France and to retreat under constant Allied attacks to the Vosges Mountains.

Operation Market Garden

Around this time the Allies launched many successful operations, too many to list here, but an unsuccessful one was Operation *Market Garden*, which took place in Holland between 17 and 25 September.

The plan was to land three airborne divisions deep behind enemy lines, the 82nd and 101st American Airborne Divisions and the 1st British Airborne Division. These would capture and hold all the bridges between the Allied front line and the town of Arnhem, where the final bridge crossed the Rhine. This would allow the ground troops of XXX Corps to push a hole through the enemy defences and advance into Germany itself.

The 1st Airborne was tasked with capturing the Arnhem Bridge, but unfortunately when they arrived the enemy strength was far greater than predicted. However, a single battalion held the northern end of the bridge against heavy attacks for three days before finally being overrun, having exhausted its ammunition. The rest of 1st Airborne was forced into a small defensive pocket at nearby Oosterbeek. The division went into battle with over 10,000 men, but only 2,100 avoided death or capture.

BATTLE OF THE BULGE

On 16 December 1944, Germany attempted its last desperate measure for success on the Western Front by using most of its remaining reserves to launch a massive counteroffensive in the Ardennes to attempt to split the Western Allies, encircle large portions of enemy troops and capture their primary supply port at Antwerp in order to force a political settlement.

Near-complete surprise was achieved by a combination of Allied overconfidence, preoccupation with their own plans and poor aerial reconnaissance. The Germans attacked a weakly defended section of the Allied line, taking advantage of heavily overcast weather conditions, which grounded Allied aircraft. But fierce resistance on the northern shoulder of the offensive around Elsenborn Ridge and in the south around Bastogne blocked German access to key roads that they needed for the operation to succeed. This and terrain that favoured the defenders threw the German advance behind schedule and allowed the Allies to reinforce the thinly spread troops. Improved weather conditions permitted air attacks on the Germans, which sealed their fate.

In the wake of the defeat, many experienced German units were left severely depleted of men and equipment, as survivors retreated to the defences of the Siegfried Line. The battle involved about 610,000 American men, of whom some 89,000 were casualties, including 19,000 killed. It was the largest and bloodiest battle fought by the United States in the Second World War.

8

1945: PEACE AND ITS CONSEQUENCES

In 1945 the most widespread conflict in history at last came to its conclusion. The war in Europe ended in May, while in Asia it continued until August. But with peace came the consequences. For instance, what would happen to the regimes that had caused the war and the evil individuals who had pursued it? What would happen to their countries and the lands they had violated? The decisions taken at that time would shape the modern world.

CLOSING IN ON TWO FRONTS

January 1945 would see the Soviets closing in on Germany from the east and the Allies approaching from the west. In the east the Germans were pushed back to the Oder River on the border between Poland and Germany itself. Then in February the Soviets invaded Silesia, a land allied to Germany which is now mainly in modern Poland but with small parts also in Czechoslovakia and Germany. They also entered Pomerania on the south shore of the Baltic Sea.

On the night of 23 March the Western Allies finally crossed the River Rhine into Germany in a coordinated set of operations around Rees and Wesel collectively known as Operation *Plunder*. It was commanded by Field Marshal Montgomery, with the British implementing operations *Turnscrew*, *Widgeon* and *Torchlight* and the Americans Operation *Flashpoint*. The crossings were mainly made in boats, while paratroopers and glider-borne units of the British 6th Airborne Division and US 17th Airborne Division conducted Operation *Varsity* by dropping on the east bank of the river.

THE YALTA CONFERENCE

The Yalta Conference was held from 4 to 11 February 1945 in the Livadia Palace near Yalta in the Crimea. It was a meeting between the government heads of the

United States, Britain and the Soviet Union. The three countries were represented by President Franklin D. Roosevelt, Prime Minister Winston Churchill and Premier Joseph Stalin respectively. Their purpose was to discuss the post-war reorganisation of Europe.

Yalta was the second of three wartime conferences at which the leaders of these great powers would meet. It was preceded by the Tehran Conference in 1943, and was followed by the Potsdam Conference in July 1945, which was attended by Stalin, Churchill and President Harry S. Truman.

THE END OF THE WAR IN EUROPE

In early April the Western Allies finally pushed forward in Italy after a long stalemate on the Gothic Line, while in Germany the race was on to reach Berlin. In the west the British and Americans were sweeping swiftly forward, and in the east Soviet and Polish forces stormed the capital in late April. American and Soviet forces would link up on the Elbe River near Torgau on 25 April.

The Battle of Berlin was the final major offensive of the European theatre. It lasted from 20 April until 2 May and was one of the bloodiest in history. The Soviets captured the Reichstag building on 30 April, which effectively brought about the military defeat of the Third Reich.

Several changes in leadership occurred during this period. On 12 April, President Roosevelt died and was succeeded by Harry Truman. Benito Mussolini was killed by Italian partisans on 28 April. With total defeat looming he had attempted to escape north, only to be quickly captured and summarily executed near Lake Como. His body was then taken to Milan, where it was hung upside down at a service station for public viewing and to provide confirmation of his demise. Two days later, Adolf Hitler committed suicide by gunshot in his bunker in Berlin. His body was afterwards burned as per his prior instructions. He was succeeded by Grand Admiral Karl Donitz.

A document entitled the German Instrument of Surrender finally brought the war in Europe to an end. It was signed on 8 May 1945 by representatives of the German Armed Forces and the Allied Expeditionary Force together with the Soviet High Command, with French and US representatives acting as witnesses. Its terms were the total and unconditional surrender of Germany. The date is known in the West as Victory in Europe Day (VE Day), whereas in post-Soviet states the victory is celebrated on 9 May, since it was signed after midnight Moscow time. In Germany, it is known as the Day of Capitulation.

Left: On 20 July 1944, German military leaders attempted to kill Adolf Hitler in the Rastenburg Assassination Plot. This photograph was taken in Munich on 8 November 1939, fifteen minutes before another failed attempt to kill the Führer when a bomb exploded in the Burgerbrau beer cellar. (Courtesy of Michael Virtue, Virtue Books)

Below: Victory in Europe Day (VE Day) was celebrated all over the United Kingdom with street parties similar to this one in Exmouth, Devon. (Courtesy of John Fletcher)

DISCOVERY OF THE NAZI CONCENTRATION CAMPS

While the Allies invaded Poland and Germany they began to discover the concentration camps where Jewish people from many parts of Europe had been taken by the Nazis as part of Hitler's Final Solution. This was the term used by the Nazis when referring to their plan of annihilating the Jewish people. The attempted genocide was the culmination of a decade of severe discriminatory measures – today called the Holocaust – when approximately 6 million Jews were murdered. The Nazis believed that the Jews were an inferior race to themselves and posed an alien threat to so-called German purity. This, at least, was the reason given to the German populace, but the confiscation of their wealth certainly provided Hitler with useful funds for his military campaigns.

The Soviets were the first to discover one of these Nazi death camps when they reached Majdanek near Lublin, Poland, in July 1944. Surprised by the rapid Soviet advance, the Germans attempted to hide the evidence of their crimes by demolishing the site. Camp personnel burned the crematorium that had been used to burn the bodies of murdered prisoners, but in their haste the gas chambers where the killings had taken place were left standing. In the summer of 1944, the Soviets also overran sites at Belzec, Sobibor, and Treblinka. The Germans had dismantled these camps in 1943, as by then most of the Jews in Poland had already been exterminated.

The largest of the concentration camps was at Auschwitz, which was liberated in January 1945. Before the Soviets arrived the Nazi guards forced most of the prisoners to march westward in what became known as the 'death marches'. When they eventually reached the camp the Russians found several thousand emaciated prisoners that had been left behind, as well as personal belongings of the victims. For example, they discovered hundreds of thousands of men's suits and more than 800,000 women's outfits.

In the following months, the Soviets liberated additional camps in the Baltic and in Poland, such as Stutthof, Sachsenhausen and Ravensbruck. In the west, US forces liberated the camps at Buchenwald, Dora-Mittelbau, Flossenburg, Dachau and Mauthausen. And the British liberated concentration camps in northern Germany, including Neuengamme and Bergen-Belsen. When they arrived at the latter in April 1945 they were confronted with the sight of 60,000 prisoners, most in critical condition because of a typhus epidemic. More than 10,000 of these would subsequently perish from the effects of malnutrition or disease within a few weeks of liberation. Here and elsewhere the liberators discovered unspeakable horrors where piles of corpses lay unburied. Only after the liberation of these camps was the full scope of Nazi atrocities exposed to the world.

Above: Gestapo chief Heinrich Himmler, second from right, was one of the main perpetrators of the Holocaust and murder of European Jews. He committed suicide by taking a cyanide pill while in British custody in May 1945. (Courtesy of Michael Virtue, Virtue Books)

Below: American sailors guard a captured harbour as the war in the Pacific nears its end. (Courtesy of Michael Virtue, Virtue Books)

TAKING BACK THE PHILIPPINES

Even though the war in Europe had ended, in Asia there was no sign of the Japanese giving up the fight, but both the Americans and the British could now bolster their presence in the area with troops that were no longer needed to combat Germany in the West.

In the Pacific Ocean at this time American operations largely centered on the Philippines. Together with Philippine forces they were steadily advancing through the islands. By the end of April they had cleared Leyte of opposition and retaken Manila after a fierce battle which reduced the city to rubble. But stubborn resistance was put up by the Japanese on Luzon, Mindanao and other islands of the group.

FIREBOMBING OF TOKYO

The Americans had first bombed Tokyo in April 1942, but the strategic bombing of the city began in 1944 after the long-range B-29 Superfortress entered service. They were first deployed from China and thereafter from the Mariana Islands. Operation *Meetinghouse*, the firebombing of Tokyo, took place from 9 to 10 March 1945. It is said to have been the single most destructive bombing raid in history.

During the raid some 330 B-29s rained incendiary bombs on the city, creating a firestorm that killed an estimated 80,000 to 100,000 people. It burned a quarter of the city to the ground and left a million people homeless.

Tokyo was the first in a series of incendiary raids launched in quick succession against the largest Japanese cities, with Nagoya, Osaka and Kobe also targeted. By the end of the war, more than sixty Japanese cities had been laid to waste by firebombing.

DROPPING THE ATOM BOMBS

In May 1945, Australian troops landed in Borneo; British, American and Chinese forces defeated the Japanese in northern Burma; and the British pushed on to reach Rangoon. Chinese forces started to counter-attack in the Battle of West Hunan that occurred between 6 April and 7 June. American forces also moved towards Japan, taking Iwo Jima by March and Okinawa by the end of June. As well as bombing Japanese cities, American submarines cut off their supply routes.

In spite of all this Japan refused to surrender, but then the Americans employed the ultimate weapon of its day. By August 1945, the Americans had developed and tested atomic bombs, and with their B-29 Superfortress the US Army Air Force had the means to deploy them from Tinian in the Mariana Islands.

In August 1945, with the approval of President Truman, the Americans dropped the first and only atomic bombs so far used in warfare. The first was dropped on the city of Hiroshima on 6 August, and the second on Nagasaki on 9 August.

Within the first two to four months of the bombings, the acute effects killed 90,000–166,000 people in Hiroshima and 60,000–80,000 in Nagasaki; roughly half of the deaths in each city occurred on the first day. During the following months, large numbers died from the effect of burns, radiation sickness, and other injuries. In both cities, most of the dead were civilians, although Hiroshima had had a sizeable garrison. The justification for employing these weapons was that the predicted death count would have been far greater if the Allies continued the war in the conventional sense and attempted to invade mainland Japan.

JAPANESE SURRENDER

Between the dropping of the two atomic bombs, the Soviets, in accordance with the Yalta Conference, declared war on Japan and invaded Japanese-held Manchuria, Sakhalin Island and the Kuril Islands. This, together with the destruction at Hiroshima and Nagasaki, left the Japanese with no other course left to them than to surrender, which they announced on 15 August. On 2 September they signed the instrument of surrender aboard the deck of the American battleship USS *Missouri* in Tokyo Harbour, officially bringing the Second World War to an end.

THE AFTERMATH OF WAR

After the war had ended the Allies established occupation administrations in Austria and Germany. The former became a neutral state, not aligned with any political bloc. The latter was divided into western and eastern occupation zones controlled by the Western Allies and the USSR respectively. Nazi politicians and military leaders were prosecuted as war criminals, with many sentenced to death.

Germany lost a quarter of its pre-war territory. Silesia, Neumark and most of Pomerania were taken over by Poland. East Prussia was divided between Poland and the USSR, followed by the expulsion of 9 million Germans from these provinces. Some 3 million Germans were also expelled from the Sudetenland in Czechoslovakia. By the 1950s, every fifth West German was a refugee from the east. The USSR annexed a large portion of eastern Poland as well as eastern

Romania, part of eastern Finland, and the Baltic states of Estonia, Latvia and Lithuania.

In Asia, the United States led the occupation of Japan and administered its former islands in the Western Pacific, while the Soviets annexed Sakhalin and the Kuril Islands. Korea, formerly under Japanese rule, was divided and occupied by the US in the south and the Soviet Union in the north. Separate republics emerged on both sides of the 38th parallel in 1948, each claiming to be the legitimate government for all of Korea, which led ultimately to the Korean War.

In China, nationalist and communist forces resumed the civil war in June 1946. Communist forces were victorious and established the People's Republic of China on the mainland, while nationalist forces retreated to Taiwan. In the Middle East, the Arab rejection of the United Nations Partition Plan for Palestine and the creation of Israel marked the escalation of the Arab–Israeli conflict. European colonial powers attempted to retain their empires, but their loss of prestige and resources during the war rendered this untenable and led to decolonisation, most importantly for Britain in India.

In an effort to maintain peace, the Allies formed the United Nations, which officially came into existence on 24 October 1945, and adopted the Universal Declaration of Human Rights in 1948 as a common standard for all member states. The great powers that were the victors of the war – the United States, Soviet Union, China, Britain, and France – formed the permanent members of the UN's Security Council and remain so to the present.

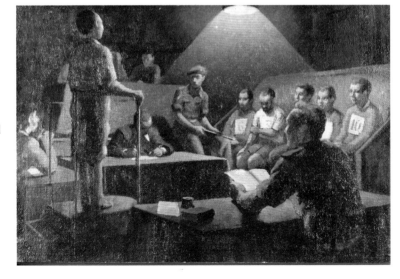

Painting in oils by Robert Strand from drawings he made during war crimes trials in Singapore in 1946. A Japanese soldier stands accused. (Author's collection)

WHAT NEXT?

TV

Band of Brothers (2001)
Dad's Army (1968–1977)
Danger UXB (1979)
Foyle's War (2002)
Holocaust (1978)
Land Girls (2009)
Nuremberg (2000)
The Pacific (2010)
The Winds of War (1983)
The World at War (1973–1974)

NOVELS/FICTION

Altman, John, *A Game of Spies*
De Bernières, Louis, *Captain Corelli's Mandolin*
Ondaatje, Michael, *The English Patient*
Harris, Robert, *Enigma*
Chabon, Michael, *The Final Solution*
Jones, James, *From Here to Eternity*
Robbins, David L., *The Last Citadel*
Beach, Edward Latimer, *Run Silent, Run Deep*

FILMS

Battle of Britain (1969)
Battle of the Bulge (1965)
The Big Red One (1980)
Bridge on the River Kwai (1957)
A Bridge Too Far (1977)
Cross of Iron (1977)
The Dam Busters (1954)
Das Boot (1981)
The Dirty Dozen (1967)
Downfall (2004)
The Great Escape (1963)
The Longest Day (1962)
Saving Private Ryan (1998)
Schindler's List (1993)
The Thin Red Line (1998)

NON-FICTION

Hastings, Max, *All Hell Let Loose*
Beevor, Antony, *The Downfall 1945*
Beevor, Antony, *The Second World War*
Beevor, Antony, *Stalingrad*
Buckton, Henry, *The Children's Front*
Buckton, Henry, *Friendly Invasion*
Gilbert, Martin, *The Holocaust: The Jewish Tragedy*
Overy, Richard, *Russia's War*

INDEX

Forthcoming Illustrated Introductions

Fascinated by history? Wish you knew more?
The Illustrated Introductions are here to help.

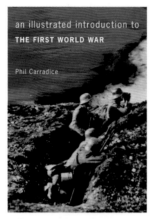

An Illustrated Introduction to the
First World War
978-1-4456-3296-4
£9.99
Available from June 2014

An Illustrated Introduction to
Ancient Egypt
978-1-4456-3365-7
£9.99
Available from July 2014

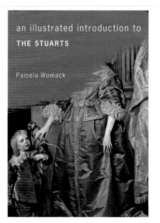

An Illustrated Introduction to the Stuarts
978-1-4456-3788-4
£9.99
Available from September 2014

Available from all good bookshops or to order direct
Please call **01453-847-800**
www.amberleybooks.com